Cristi Puiu

Contemporary Film Directors

Edited by Justus Nieland and Jennifer Fay

The Contemporary Film Directors series provides concise, well-written introductions to directors from around the world and from every level of the film industry. Its chief aims are to broaden our awareness of important artists, to give serious critical attention to their work, and to illustrate the variety and vitality of contemporary cinema. Contributors to the series include an array of internationally respected critics and academics. Each volume contains an incisive critical commentary, an informative interview with the director, and a detailed filmography.

A list of books in the series appears at the end of this book.

Cristi Puiu

Monica Filimon

UNIVERSITY OF ILLINOIS PRESS
URBANA, CHICAGO, AND SPRINGFIELD

1 2 3 4 5 C P 5 4 3 2 1
∞ This book is printed on acid-free paper.

All photographs taken by Silvana Bratu.
Stills © Mandragora
Frontispiece: Cristi Puiu on the set of *The Death of Mr. Lazarescu* (2005)

Library of Congress Cataloging-in-Publication Data
Names: Filimon, Monica, 1976– author.
Title: Cristi Puiu / by Monica Filimon.
Description: Urbana : University of Illinois Press, 2017. | Series: Contemporary film directors | Includes bibliographical references and index.
Identifiers: LCCN 2016035731| ISBN 9780252040764 (hardcover : alk. paper) | ISBN 9780252082276 (pbk. : alk. paper) | ISBN 9780252099205 (e-book)
Subjects: LCSH: Puiu, Cristi, 1967- —Criticism and interpretation.
Classification: LCC PN1998.3.P8535 F55 2017 | DDC 791.4302/33092—dc23
LC record available at https://lccn.loc.gov/2016035731

Contents

Acknowledgments | ix

INEFFABLE EXPERIENCES OF THE PROFANE WORLD | 1

The Ineffable and the Profane 1

Au revoir, les communistes? 13

Theater of Memory: *The Retirement Home* 27

The Road Not Taken: *Stuff and Dough* 39

Fathers and Sons: *Cigarettes and Coffee* 50

Regarding the Death of Others: *The Death of Mr. Lazarescu* 58

Author! Author! *Aurora* 72

Masks Off! *Three Exercises of Interpretation* 96

What's in a Name? "Das Spektrum Europas" 107

Father Is Gone: *Sieranevada* 116

INTERVIEW WITH CRISTI PUIU | 123

Filmography | 151

Bibliography | 155

Index | 165

Acknowledgments

The writing of this book would not have been possible without the help of many dear friends, as well as the financial and logistical support of several institutions. I would like to thank them for their confidence in this project and their kind assistance to me during its realization.

When I started my research into the origins and evolution of the New Romanian Cinema, one of the first companies I contacted was Mandragora; their openness to dialogue was unique among the many other production houses and institutions with which I corresponded at the time. I am very grateful to director Cristi Puiu for his generosity of spirit, patience, and the many hours of engaging, thought-provoking conversation about cinema. I would also like to thank producer Anca Puiu for her gracious support, and Raluca Păduraru for her promptness and professionalism.

Jennifer Fay's and Justus Nieland's insightful, stimulating comments have been instrumental in conferring a more coherent focus and structure upon the project. Daniel Nasset's very prompt responses and help have made the drafting process easy and smooth. I thank them all for a wonderful experience.

Writing demands a specific commitment of one's time and attention. My colleagues at Kingsborough Community College, CUNY have made it all possible for me. Provost Stuart Suss's help and encouragement, as well as President Farley Herzek's support for my work, have enabled me to stay focused and motivated. Professor Eileen Ferretti's wise advice and constant trust in me have energized and stimulated me. I am very grateful to all.

Support for this project was also provided by a PSC-CUNY Award, jointly funded by The Professional Staff Congress and The City University of New York. I would like to thank Wanda Morales, Antonio Thompson, and Carmen Rodriguez, at Kingsborough Community College, CUNY, who streamlined the process of writing and applying for the grant, and made the experience very rewarding.

No person travels alone, and I am particularly lucky to have been accompanied by many experienced minds on my journey. Professor Stuart Liebman's astute observations, critical suggestions, and patience have been crucial to the entire drafting process. Professor Robert Singer has offered insightful comments and unwavering encouragement for many years. My intellectual growth and critical judgment have been nurtured by my former professors at Rutgers University, especially Susan Martin-Márquez, Fatima Naqvi, and Alan Williams, and Jerry Carlson at the Graduate Center, CUNY. I am deeply indebted to them all. I would also like to thank Gary Crowdus and his editorial colleagues at *Cineaste Magazine* for their constant intellectual engagement with the New Romanian Cinema and their support for my own writing.

My project has greatly benefited from the suggestions and comments I have received during my participation at various conferences and from the many different conversations I have had with film scholars and professionals. Lenuta Giukin, Ileana Marin, Otilia Baraboi, and Maria Sabina Draga Alexandru have made insightful comments that provided depth and range to my project. Mihai Chirilov's and Corina Șuteu's invaluable information about the Romanian film industry and cinema culture have been crucial to my understanding of the field. I would like to express my deep appreciation to all of them. I would also like to thank Dr. Nathan Waxman, Susu Durst, and Daniel Larson for their support and encouragement.

My friends and family have given me the strength and nourished my enthusiasm to pursue my interests. I would like to thank Lia Ungureanu, Raluca and Dorin Bîrzu, Laura Crăciunoiu, Hugo Rios, Joshua Beall, and Federica Franze for their friendship and advice. I am profoundly grateful to my parents Eugenia and Bogdan for their love and unwavering confidence in me; to my sister Stefania, her husband Liviu, and their children Robert and Eva, for their patience and understanding; and to my grandparents Silvia and Ștefan for providing me with the historical consciousness and passion for cinema that cannot be learned from books.

Cristi Puiu

Ineffable Experiences of the Profane World

The Ineffable and the Profane

"I do not think that realism exists; it is merely a label," claims director Cristi Puiu every time interviewers venture to use the term in relation to his work.[1] Yet realism would be the first qualifier most critics would associate with his films, especially with the groundbreaking *Moartea domnului Lăzărescu* (The Death of Mr. Lazarescu; 2005). The Romanian himself is not a stranger to the discussions surrounding the philosophical underpinnings of cinematic realism. As a student of the École Supérieure d'Arts Visuels in Geneva, Puiu titled his thesis "Notes sur une poétique du cinéma réaliste," and conceived it in dialogue with Robert Bresson's *Notes sur le cinématographe* and Bertold Brecht's *A Short Organum for the Theater* (Puiu, "Manifest" 97). His very emergence as one of the innovative contemporary voices in filmmaking created controversies in his native country precisely for its too-realistic depiction of life on the outskirts of a metropolis. Released at Cannes, *Marfa și banii* (Stuff and Dough; 2001), his debut feature, received laudatory reviews abroad (Chirilov and Sandu 54). In Bucharest, however, many of the old-time critics found it too unrefined, aesthetically clumsy, and vulgar in language (Chirilov and Sandu 52–53; Șerban, *4 decenii* 76). Most notoriously, *Mr. Lazarescu* was initially denied state funding only to be celebrated once it had won the Un Certain Regard award, the first important prize for a Romanian feature since 1965. Its twenty-four-hour plot, long takes, handheld camera, dark humor, naturalistic acting, and focus on the drama of an ordinary individual—all attributes of cinematic realism—would become a trademark of the New Romanian Cinema (henceforth NRC), bringing into the spotlight a country whose films had never been included in any canon.[2]

Puiu's "method," however, seems to elude clear-cut description as his own films swerve adroitly among several forms of expression, from classical shot-reverse shot montage to long takes, from raw to multiply framed shots, and from a nervous, handheld camera to a distant, fixed "eye." His third feature, *Aurora* (2010), relied on a more stylized version of his documentary-style approach, and has been, for many, a puzzle. There is a tension between the unadulterated, straightforward rendering of the observed world and the exposure of the reconstructed, fictional nature of the universe on screen that is at the core of his preoccupations, much more so than for any other Romanian filmmaker. Nevertheless, the faithful depiction of the surrounding world is, I will suggest, only an effect, and not the goal, of Puiu's endeavors. His cinema seeks to inspire viewers' brief epiphanies about the sacred dimension of the profane world. The director characterizes these experiences as "ineffable" and bemoans the gradual desensitization of the secular world toward the spiritual realm that lies beyond it. His films are, therefore, to be experienced rather than watched; they touch, provoke, and unsettle viewers.

For many, Puiu himself remains a difficult man to pin down. Driven and passionately defending his own perspective in any conversation, he appears rough and contrarian. This is only a superficial impression. He is highly perceptive of his interlocutor's mood, enthusiastic about books, films, and ideas, and generous with those around him. He describes himself as the product of a direct encounter with History, spurred by the unprecedented overhaul of politics, memory, and identity in the wake of 1989. In a sense, he is the opposite of the ex-communist subject, for whom performance—at work, in the street, and even at home—was a survival tactic. Years of communist repression had led families to withdraw within their shells and distrust everybody else, as surreal images of unity and prosperity kept rolling on screens. Puiu came of age in a land of the absurd, populated by people increasingly exiled from each other, a condition he resented.

The December 1989 events were a shock. Nicolae Ceaușescu's execution, the hidden snipers shooting at the hundreds of street protestors, and the panic created by repeated public announcements of potential terrorist attacks across the country plunged citizens into contradictory states of mind that ran the gamut from enthusiasm to fear and suspicion. Many believed that a radical change had been effected; others, Puiu among them, tried to prevent the neo-communists from taking over. Disillusionment followed the euphoria of "revolution," while concern for the other, never fully cultivated in communism, diminished even further.

It was the other Europe, spared of decades of totalitarianism, that would fashion Puiu into a filmmaker. In Geneva, he had more freedom to experiment and better access to a rich, diverse cinema culture than the one provided at the time by the National University of Theater and Film "I. L. Caragiale" in Bucharest. His immediate affinity for John Cassavetes's work eventually determined his orientation toward direct cinema. Filmmakers such as Robert Bresson, Jean Eustache, Eric Rohmer, Raymond Depardon, and Frederick Wiseman further consolidated his preference for an unembellished, sharp rendering of the minutiae of everyday life.

Upon Puiu's return to Romania in 1996, his first instinct was to document life. Cinema, he believed early in his career, was a "technique for the investigation of reality" (Puiu, "Manifest" 99). It was not an end in itself, but a means to an end. "Filmmakers use cinema as a tool, like [a] scientist's instrument," he commented in a later interview; "[t]hey ask questions about human existence, human nature, and the world. The camera is an anthropological instrument" (Puiu, "Interview"). Puiu, however, only codirected one documentary, *13–19 iulie, Craiova, Azilul de batrâni* (July 13th–July 19th, Craiova, The Retirement Home; 1998), a moving radiography of an institution inspired by Frederick Wiseman, and shot in a *cinéma vérité* style. His second project in the same vein was undertaken in collaboration with visual artist Ștefan Constantinescu, and it was an expression of concern for a different category of people: the victims of the Romanian gulag. Titled *Archive of Pain* (2000), the video installation consisted of a few metal structures, organized as prison cells, in which extended interviews with former political prisoners were projected for the itinerant visitor. The interviews were recorded on VHS tapes, an affordable medium at the time and one that was, symbolically, connected to resistance to propaganda even during communism, when the latest American films were available on such tapes and only behind closed doors.[3] For Puiu, the *Archive* was a very personal engagement with questions of memory, identity, and collective responsibility that preoccupy him to this day.

The suffering of the other, confined within the decaying walls of an institution or of traumatic memory itself, was not easy to witness, and he soon abandoned it. Documentary filmmaking, he believes, is an intrusion into people's lives and not necessarily more revelatory than fiction. The "documentary treatment of fiction" may be more effective, he came to believe (Puiu, "Manifest" 99). The majority of his critics have focused on this aspect of his directing, particularly new in Romania, and poignantly unsettling even for international cinema buffs, well versed in similar attempts by directors such as Chantal Akerman, Abbas Kiarostami, or Pedro Costas.

"Minimalism" was the first label Romanian critics associated with Puiu's work. The late Alex. Leo Șerban, the leading figure at the time, argued that *Stuff and Dough* established a certain "minimalist" canon for those interested in a new aesthetic: films were to be made on a low budget; the camera was to be handheld; the sound was to be recorded on location; and the plot was to avoid the "artifice" associated with "traditional" cinema (that is, old Romanian cinema) (Șerban, *4 decenii* 56–57). Angelo Mitchievici linked the NRC "minimalism" (which he also traced back to Puiu's first feature) to André Bazin, the French New Wave, and the Danish Dogma 95 (52). In his opinion, a new form of realism—devoid of "revolutionary spirit" and "ideological positioning," and relying on a "randomized," decentered, subjective perspective—constitutes the core of this new minimalism (53). More recently, in the first study of the Romanian cinema published in English, Dominique Nasta contends that *Mr. Lazarescu*'s "minimalist aesthetics" can include, well, everything: "long shots," "lateral framing," "minute scrutiny of everyday, often non-spectacular details," the absence of a musical soundtrack, the "challenging of audience emotional participation," the "lack of ellipses," the "everyday small talk," the impression of "documentary 'life shooting'," and the subdued acting (157). Minimalism was, therefore, eventually employed to refer to all that was novel in Puiu's and, by erroneous extension, in the entire NRC legacy. Critics mostly related it to his style, but conflated artistic and thematic choices, and, more importantly, spent little space discussing the origins and philosophical implications of the term, Puiu's own pursuits, or the major differences among the NRC directors. Minimalism roughly describes a tendency to eliminate all possible "attractions"—stylistic flourishes, idiosyncratic expressions, and complex composition—to encourage the viewer to ponder the nature of the artistic object and the means through which it reaches its public (Varendoe 3). Puiu does opt for a certain aesthetic sobriety, but, as I shall suggest, his stylistic choices and *mise en scène* are less straightforward than they may seem. Most importantly, his interest is not in "the cinematic as 'simple' art object," but in the revelations it may invite (Pop 68).

The director's cinema philosophy has also been defined in relation to André Bazin's theories. In the first book to devote ample space to his influence on the NRC, Romanian critic Andrei Gorzo underscores Puiu's preference for real-time duration, complex characters, and depth (of field, off-screen space, or psychological structures) (*Lucruri* 218, 245, 255). I would argue that Puiu is, at heart, a documentary filmmaker increasingly interested in the act of observation and what it can yield to the observer. His camera does not merely open a window onto the world, but draws attention to the very physical act of perception, to its limits, and to what it may leave beyond. Constant framing supplements its effect. Corridors, doorways, and windows reduce viewers' field of vision, while characters' accounts of others emphasize the incomplete nature of storytelling, as does the films' dependence on relatively long takes and clearly marked cuts (to underscore the lapse in time and information). Puiu's is always a much larger world filtered through the sensibility of an absent other.

Furthermore, I will suggest that, especially in his first films, the camera, in its movement, conveys a haptic sense of the space it inhabits, thereby prompting viewers' corporeal responsiveness as well as a more engaged type of seeing than one may expect. The rather impressionistic use of color and surfaces also influences perception. These "visceral" qualities of the image and the overall approach of the subject matter reflect, in Jim Hoberman's opinion, a posttraumatic hysteria about the limits of representation in an age in which live broadcast of terrorist attacks have toppled the Hollywood imagination factory (31–32). One could argue that the televised events of December 1989 had the same shock value for Romanian viewers.[4] Films, the American critic writes, have become "experiential," that is, as close to the real-life experience of the "event" on screen as possible (Hoberman 29, 32). I would suggest that the "experiential" quality of Puiu's early films, particularly of *Mr. Lazarescu*, is not primarily motivated by a search for a gut-wrenching response to the worries of the times, nor is it triggered by his interest in the Bazinian myth of total cinema. Puiu's close faithfulness to experience is grounded in his faith that it may prompt unexpected glimpses at what resides beyond the observable, and this may explain the stylistic differences among his films.

By the 2000s, the director had already decided in favor of fiction cinema. The world around him had also changed radically. The gap between the haves and have-nots in Romania had widened and many had immigrated to make their fortunes elsewhere. The strong familial ties of the dying traditional society were now beginning to break as the old and the new worlds coexisted and clashed. Romania joined the European Union (henceforth EU) on January 1, 2007, with great hopes of economic prosperity, only to find itself at an impasse after the 2008 financial crisis. Puiu's rise to international visibility thus roughly parallels the increasing disappearance of borders within Europe and at large, and the radical reconfiguration of people's knowledge as the electronic world expanded.

The nature of human communication or of an individual's relationship with the surrounding reality, and the role of cinema in the new age, are central to the director's investigations today. No longer merely a way of observing and reconstructing one's immediate experience, filmmaking has become a means of confession, the art of laying one's soul bare to an Other.[5] Puiu's "confessions," recent critics have suggested, are governed by very specific "procedures." In probably the most thorough study of the NRC to date, Doru Pop confers upon the director the (implied) title of a prophet for his kin (43). His "cinematic Gospel," Pop argues, is built around four principles: "immediate realism" (or present-tense narration); "truthful naturalism" (or the slice-of-life inspiration for his plots); "involved authenticity" (or the fidelity to life "as it happens" at a moment of crisis); and "social responsibility" (or the exposure of "moral issues" and the "depths" of the human condition) (43–46, 52). Such a description implies that Puiu's foremost interest is in the method rather than the explorations he undertakes in his films. Furthermore, the qualities Pop attributes to his cinema can be applied to many other NRC films. Christian Ferencz-Flatz's more recent phenomenological investigation of the documentary impulse in Puiu's cinema adds the director's desire that his films generate knowledge to Pop's list. In this respect, fiction, much like real-life experiences, is equally valuable (Ferencz-Flatz 27, 112–13). The critic, however, stops short of exploring the type of knowledge Puiu seeks, or the deeper motivations and intricacies of his texts. I would suggest that one of the director's goals is to establish a connection with his viewers based on a sense of shared experience. Such a moment can only be obtained when one's confession is stripped of all tendencies to exaggerate the telling and manipulate the audience. Puiu's "rules" are, therefore, a function, and not the center, of his philosophy.

It is, therefore, the aim of this study to shed light on some of the Romanian filmmaker's predispositions and explorations, as they are embodied in his texts. I will suggest that his cinema seeks to inspire, in viewers, what he terms the "ineffable," or a sense of the sacred dimension of the profane world. Puiu's religious convictions play a part in his philosophy of cinema. He believes in God as a mysterious force whose hovering presence can be felt in the complexity of the natural world and the depth of the human mind; it is a God that remains unacknowledged and ignored by his modern-day "children." The fraught relationships between fathers and sons, obsessively pursued in all his films, is, primarily, a reaction to Puiu's experience of history, but it is also to be understood from this religious perspective. Romanian Orthodoxy, a form of Greek Orthodoxy, has a long tradition of mystical writings, and Puiu seems particularly attracted to the more recent diaries and memoirs of clerics who suffered in the communist prisons and overcame their harrowing experiences. The "ineffable" may refer to the revelation of God, but,

I would argue, it points to a much larger, different dimension of one's earthly existence. Romanian historian of religions Mircea Eliade defined it as "a reality of a wholly different order from 'natural' realities" that was very much present for the religious individual of the archaic societies, but is completely lost for today's citizens of the Western world (10–12). The sacred is a "mode of being in the world," an "absolute reality" that transcends one's daily experiences, makes possible the communication between mortals and deities, and gives purpose and meaning to one's life (Eliade 14, 21).

Puiu is, or seeks to become, such a religious man, and he bemoans ordinary individuals' blindness to forces larger than themselves. He is fascinated with the significance of death, which he increasingly believes to be merely a transitional phase. In *Stuff and Dough,* the death of others possibly triggers the revelation of the absolute evil for the protagonist. Lazarescu's impending death may, similarly, draw viewers' attention to the other realm, to which he travels, and to their own mortality. In *Aurora,* the protagonist becomes an agent of death, a man who, implicitly, sees himself as God in a world that has lost its spiritual moorings. *Sieranevada* (2016), his latest feature, depicts an empty commemoration of death, as survivors spend little time pondering the fate of the deceased. People talk past, and do not hear, each other. Puiu suggests that, in a desacralized world, one's death becomes an end rather than a passing, and good and evil cannot be easily recognized; there is no redemption or salvation for those blind by choice. His films thus call for an urgent self-examination of one's place in the world and deep connections with everybody else around.

Author, actors, and viewers need to prepare for such revelation of the sacred. A director, Puiu believes, should "wonder" at the world, rather than make statements about it, in order to enter into "resonance" with it and develop a certain acuity of perception for "that which cannot be put into words" (Puiu, "An Interview" 9, 15). In their turn, actors should abandon any extraneous thought of the reality beyond the set, and be present "then and there," fully engaged in the moment. Viewers themselves need to be open to discover something of which they are not yet aware; they must put themselves "in the listening position." Finally, the film is to remain as close as possible to the empirically observed world and to the manner in which it is experienced so that it can preserve, within it, the conditions for the "ineffable" to emerge (Puiu, "Interviu"). The "ineffable" is, thus, a moment of grace, when all engaged recognize something that is bigger than the moment (be it the moment of acting/directing, or of watching) and that gives them insight into their own condition as mortal human beings connected to each other in their vulnerability. "We are wretched human beings," comments Mr. Lazarescu in the ambulance that carries him, like a hearse, to his final destination; Puiu's cinema echoes him.

It is, therefore, not surprising that his films, with few exceptions, rely on a second, allegorical level, borrowed from religion, fairy tales, and myth, to highlight the universality of their historically grounded plots. The surreptitious presence of Evil disguised as a small-time crook in *Stuff and Dough;* Mr. Lazarescu's travels through the Purgatory of the health-care system in Bucharest; and Viorel's multiple identities as "wolf," "hunter," and fallen savior provide several such opportunities for viewers to meditate on the unexpected, deeper significance of mundane encounters. Furthermore, narratives are organized as failed journeys of initiation, in which protagonists remain ultimately blind to the parallel existential dimension with which they cross paths.

To highlight the complexity of today's world, Puiu's films also pay very close attention to the intricate details of an individual's interactions with others. Protagonists are impossibly ambiguous, as one objectionable trait is redeemed by an act of kindness or love for another. The insistence on almost real-time duration and on plots that focus on a day or so in a person's life allows for the open-endedness of all details woven into the story, from characters who are either never seen or never named, to actions that do not fit any narrative "purpose," yet take up a significant portion of the screen time. There is a "thickness" of information that becomes, to some degree, overwhelming, conferring upon the screen world its mystery. Cinema is, in this respect, the means for a constant return to the world and the Other, in wonder and with love.

Titled "Au revoir, les communistes?" the first section of this essay is a brief examination of the political, social, and cultural environment that preceded and informed Puiu's artistic and moral credo. I suggest that, during the transition from communism to postcommunism, there was more continuity than disruption between the power structures, the individuals who populated them, and their practices. In the 1990s, "children" (the young men and women who went out in the streets in 1989) would constantly battle against "fathers" who kept their hold on power. Romanian historian Lucian Boia and American anthropologist Katherine Verdery provide critical instruments for the examination of post-1989 history as one of coexistent contradictory dispositions masked by the inflated narratives of freedom and democracy. The result was not only a stark deterioration of all types of economic protection, with disastrous effects on most cultural sectors, cinema in particular, but also a dramatic reduction of citizens' trust in the state's moral and social authority. The world seemed disjointed. When carefully examined, loud, angry condemnations of communism were merely simulated on television shows and largely blocked any authentic examination of the past. A man of his times, Puiu would react vehemently to what he deemed to be the disingenuousness of public discourses and gestures.

In *The Retirement Home,* codirectors Andreea Păduraru and Puiu would expose the dishonesty of such empty denunciations and would seek to understand the dying world of the elderly, as the second section of this volume, "Theater of Memory," indicates. Their documentary takes an affectionate look at one of the few remaining institutions for senior care at the time. The "inmates" are the last surviving wards of the communist state, and their traumas, memories, and bewilderment with the new are revealed as candid relationships to the world. They are "grandparents" whose time has passed. Central to the filmmakers' approach is the vivid rendering of decaying bodies and spaces, symbolically replicated at the level of people's memories and articulated narrative. The haptic quality of the image, explored through Giuliana Bruno's theoretical lens, generates viewers' direct, bodily response, empathetic with human suffering. Păduraru and Puiu further rely on the subtle observation of the solidarity established not only within the Home, but also between the camera and its "subjects" in order to indicate the concrete means through which people relate to each other in private spaces, away from the scrutiny of postcommunist media. What could have been a clinical investigation of an institution eventually digresses into the narrative flow of nostalgia, and history becomes a very personal journey back to times gone and people departed.

Puiu's first feature *Stuff and Dough* focuses on a different generation: the young and the rash, full of dreams and lost in illusions of absolute potency. With the help of Guy Standing's analysis of postindustrial classes, "The Road Not Taken," the third section of this essay, explores the effects of incipient capitalism on one of the most vulnerable categories of urban dwellers, the "precariat" (1–2). Not quite qualified for the new world, the youth and the discarded employees of closing factories are left without their proper space within the city and its economy. In between an impotent father and a malefic one, Puiu's protagonist makes a fatal choice: a pact with the Devil (revealed here to be the middle man between the underground world of crime and the nouveaux riches of capitalism). To make the film, Puiu chose "the road not taken" in Romanian cinema and refused major concessions; *Stuff and Dough* suffered the consequences. At odds with all local "favorites" (the still-popular films of the pre-1989 era; the "hysterical" cinema of the 1990s; and Hollywood blockbusters), it refused an easy answer to the dilemmas it posed, and enlisted a handheld camera as a partial witness, thereby jolting viewers' perception. The repeated undermining of the road movie genre expectations, the subjective restriction of the visual field, and the absence of stylistic "ornaments" (whether spectacular camera movements and editing, or a non-diegetic musical soundtrack, for example) transformed the viewing experience into a constant interrogation of the protagonist's choices. The establishment dismissed the film's compassionate observation of the fate of the precariat classes as the work of an inexperienced director. Puiu would not relent.

In his next work, the short *Un cartuş de Kent şi un pachet de cafea* (Cigarettes and Coffee; 2004), he would place full center the troubled relationship between generations. "Fathers and Sons," the fourth section, examines Puiu's nuanced, yet aesthetically sober depiction of characters' blindness to the deeper ties that unite them. In spite of his many confrontations with the "fathers" of Romanian cinema, the young director took a sympathetic look at the older generation, portrayed here as weak, yet dignified. Classical editing, the theatricality of some of the frames, and the film's reliance on repetition confer upon it the cutting-edge simplicity and insight of an early cinema production. Viewers are invited to engage with the conundrums of their time, and observe the draining away of affection that could have bridged the otherwise tense generational divide.

The same narrative and aesthetic scalpel would reveal the burdens of old age as postcommunism meets globalism, and both give little respite to Mr. Lazarescu, the anonymous city dweller. In "Regarding the Death of Others," I suggest that the anthropologist's eye for "thick description" and the film's relative stylistic austerity become the conditions for viewers' epiphany about an individual's solitude before death (Geertz 10). As families disintegrate, sons and daughters move away, ailing parents are left to fend for themselves, and genuine human connection is severely threatened. "Witnessing without the taint of artistry" is crucial for the film's tender look at the other's pain, Puiu also suggests (Sontag 26). The sober, yet complex ethnographic and symbolic reconstruction of a milieu offers the director the necessary space to explore the difficulty of finding and giving grace in most troublesome circumstances. The film screens all information through the capricious perception of the observational camera, thereby examining the significance of the silent witness in the modern world. Furthermore, Puiu subtly emphasizes one's epistemological and emotional constraints, suggested through framing, marked temporal lapses in the otherwise real-time duration of the events, and the slow, incremental accumulation of crucial information through repetition. Viewers' ultimate empathy with the protagonist urges them to reflect upon their own vulnerability and possible loneliness.

Puiu's search for an epiphany about the human beings on screen becomes more poignant with *Aurora*. "Author! Author!" is an analysis into the makings of an author, be it the author of a murder or the author of a text, in a desacralized world. This sixth section appeals to various cultural critics to give shape to the many "ghosts" haunting the film: that of the invisible violence built within the new market economy and the repressed anger it generates; that of a dead father and of his murderous son; and, at a self-reflexive level, that of an implied, metaphysical author hovering over the text. More than Puiu's previous works, *Aurora* stands out for the richness of its description, as *mise en scène,* props, diegetic music, and characters' choice of words acquire symbolical significance. Viewers' access to the protagonist's world is constantly constrained (through narrative ellipses and omissions, restrictive framing, and a fixed camera observer), so the text draws progressive attention to its ephemeral condition as a socially, historically, and culturally grounded work. Puiu's intention is that such heightened awareness of a film's limited, "human" condition may, eventually, inspire viewers to question that which has remained unseen and unspoken: the "ineffable" of a world beyond one's immediate grasp.

The question of authorship is also central to the next section, "Masks Off!" which examines a workshop production titled *Trois exercices d'interprétation* (Three Exercises of Interpretation; 2011). Puiu searches for the invisible connection with the viewer, a connection made possible only through a shared epiphany of human limits and the larger world to which they bar access. Such a transference of vision between a film and its spectators can be temporarily achieved only when the actors let go of their "masks," stay present in the moment, and are attuned to each other in front of the camera. Puiu's theories of acting are reminiscent of David Mamet's, but the Romanian adds an extra ingredient (not new to his understanding of cinema): love. Love (for the part and the viewer) and trust (in the director) are the premises for removing the "mask" and revealing the fragile human being behind it.

Masks, and the many labels people attach to each other, are also exposed as the barriers to genuine communication and connection in "Das Spektrum Europas," a short included in *Les Ponts de Sarajevo* (Bridges of Sarajevo; 2014). Intended as a cultural *lieu de memoire* for the new, united Europe, the omnibus film questions the superficial veneer of official discourses that seek to bury discord and discontent deep under the rug. Puiu incisively exposes the continuing legacy of nationalism, xenophobia, and anti-Semitism that profoundly marked the twentieth century and isolated people within comfortable, yet dysfunctional worlds.

Cinema is a confession about the road one has walked and witnessed, Puiu firmly believes. It is not any confession, however. It demands rigor, acuity of spirit and perception, self-discipline, and the often-distressing act of acknowledging one's own deficiencies and mortality. It is not a cinema for the weak-hearted.

Au revoir, les communistes?

In 2012, when Romanian historian Lucian Boia published an extended essay entitled *Why Is Romania Different?* he could not have predicted its impact among his compatriots. Selling more than forty thousand copies, the book was republished in a second edition one year later, when it ignited an intense debate about what many had perceived as the denigration of the country and its history. Boia argues that Romania, situated at the crossroads of several empires, has cultivated a culture of compromise rather than one of resistance and ethical consistency (86). Moral compromise was at the core of Romanian politics in the first two decades after the fall of the Iron Curtain, when the refusal to confront and take responsibility for the past ensured the ex–Communist Party officials a comfortable grip on power. Resistance, however, was only around the corner. The NRC was born in opposition to such moral compromise, and some of its roots lie in Cristi Puiu's relentless pursuit of his own vision of cinema.

Boia is not the only historian to note that Romania is different, in a fundamental way, from its European counterparts (Judt 622). Today, much of this difference is attributed to its particular communist history, always at odds with the "trends" of similar regimes, especially during Ceaușescu's twenty-five-year "dynasty." Cristi Puiu was born only two years into this regime, at a time when hopes for a more Western-oriented socialist system were still high (Judt 623; Verdery 31–33; Kotkin 27–30). Ceaușescu opposed the 1968 Soviet invasion of Prague, and decided to pay off Romania's foreign debt when all other Eastern European countries were borrowing money to satisfy their populations' needs. With the 1970s international energy and financial crises, the communist economic system entered its moribund stage. As Katherine Verdery underlines, years of rigid centralized planning led only to severe shortages and distressed consumers (20–22). The result was a parallel, underground economic network that robbed the state, undermined its authority, and imposed a clear separation between the haves (the Party apparatchiks, Milovan Djilas's "new class" or Stephen Kotkin's "uncivil society") and the have-nots (the rest of the population), "them" and "us" (Verdery 40; Djilas 37–39; Kotkin 12–15). The intermediaries between "them" and "us" gained a lot of money and influence, and the character of Marcel Ivanov in Puiu's *Stuff and Dough* is one of them.

As the atomization of society intensified, Ceaușescu veered dramatically toward the re-Stalinization of the country, which led, in turn, to its extreme isolationism capped by a gaudy cult of personality, while most other regimes opened up spaces of contestation within the public sphere in anticipation of imminent changes (see Tismaneanu 187–233; Deletant 173–255; Djilas 38–40). In Romania, surveillance and repression deepened, breaking apart the already feeble opposition (Boia, *De ce* 106; Verdery 42; Tismaneanu 294). Mass penury and fear dominated the late 1980s, when Romanians stood in line for bread and meat, withdrew into unheated apartments, looked over their shoulders, and waited.

Probably the most enduring effect of communism was its remapping of the human spirit. Historians have commented on the direct dependence created between the ordinary citizen and the paternalistic state, whose strong hand in both rewarding and disciplining its "children" transformed them into obedient, largely passive receptors of ideology (Verdery 25–26; Boia, *România* 164). Fathers kept silent in front of the Father himself: Ceaușescu and his many representatives. Starting in the 1960s, a widespread campaign to build new industries, and the urbanization that accompanied it, as well as relatively important investments in education, allowed the Romanian state to promise a new, less burdensome life to millions of ex-villagers who, for the first time, could enjoy the advantages of modern living (minimal in Romania compared to other Eastern European countries, but quite a change from the rather primitive amenities in the villages at the time) (Deletant 166–68). Puiu's parents belong to this first-generation urban citizenry; his mother, a primary-school teacher, and his father, a functionary in a Bucharest hospital, worked long hours to ensure a decent living for their three children (the director has a sister and a brother). The disillusionment, impotence, and precarious existence of the newly created working classes after 1989 would be central to the NRC, particularly to Puiu's sensitive eye to irony and social injustice.

When the mirage of communal living wore off and shortages of all types piled up in the 1980s, an elaborate nationalist mythology diverted some of the masses' attention away from their daily frustrations; the strategy was to endure well into the 1990s, whenever the establishment felt it was losing control (Boia, *De ce* 101; Boia, *History and Myth* 75–76). Finally, the increasingly restricted and, eventually, forbidden public expression of any affect except patriotism produced what Anikó Imre has termed "traumatic citizenship," a form of repression that slowly simmered within the private sphere until it could no longer hold ("Global Media" 247).

Cinema was at the forefront of the communist cultural policies. After the nationalization of the few studios in 1948, the state maintained full monopoly over film production, distribution, and exhibition. By the 1960s, it had built some of the most lavish studios in Eastern Europe for a smooth "line-manufacturing" of cultural products throughout the 1970s and 1980s (Uricaru 430). Moralizing comedies, social dramas, and national epics about grand leaders promoted an idealized vision of a balanced, courageous, and noble people (Popescu 241–48). As economic conditions deteriorated, some films critiqued the corruption and incompetence of a few Party members, but they were only the state's controlled attempt at relieving social pressure (Popescu 257). Shot in a quasi socialist-realist style, which combined classical editing with an aestheticized, yet often bland, *mise en scène* and an emotional musical soundtrack, these films were visually and thematically facile propaganda.

A brief relaxation of the censorship at the beginning of the 1980s made room for auteur filmmaking.[6] Directors such as Mircea Daneliuc, Lucian Pintilie, Alexandru Tatos, Dan Pița, and Stere Gulea were able to release films that opposed the regime-endorsed aesthetics; they were, at the time, the "heroes" of then-teenage Puiu, Cristian Mungiu, and Radu Muntean. Daneliuc's *Probă de microfon* (Microphone Test; 1980) and *Croaziera* (The Cruise; 1981) featured protagonists whose impulses and desires were a far cry from the communist model heroes; they are among the most quoted as favorites by NRC directors. Pintilie's *De ce trag clopotele, Mitică?* (Why Are the Bells Ringing, Mitica?; 1981), a film whose release was forbidden, and Tatos's *Secvențe* (Sequences; 1982) focused on the very act of filmmaking, turning their cameras on the profoundly corrupted society of the period. Pița's *Concursul* (The Competition; 1982) and *Faleze de nisip* (Sand Cliffs; 1983), forbidden at the time, also included rebel figures who, unlike the socialist models, seemed to be doing nothing all day only to fall prey to unscrupulous, rapacious, always older men (as was Ceaușescu by 1983). Romanian critic and journalist Cristian Tudor Popescu argues that much of these films' discourse, however, reinforced communist ideology: the corrupted were always the bourgeois, intellectual figures easy to identify in official propaganda (271). Nevertheless, their visual metaphors, indirect criticism of the regime, and *double entendres* thrilled Romanian viewers, already versed in reading between the lines.

The tension between the concrete, unembellished, morally adrift society of auteur cinema and the heroic, model society of official propaganda grew throughout the 1980s. Romanians watched films looking for any anti-Party slip; the Party did the same. This chase produced a highly cryptic cinema by 1989. Initially, directors focused on contemporary realities and constructed complex characters, avoiding the moralizing, didactic tone and denouements of entertainment cinema. *Microphone Test* and *Sequences* belong to this era. After 1983, filmmakers became more ideologically conventional in their approach to theme, plot, and character construction, but continued to include visual and, especially, verbal anti-regime puns, as did Daneliuc in *Glissando* (1984), and Stere Gulea in *Morometții* (The Moromete Family; 1987). When censorship tightened, directors withdrew into allusion, parable, metaphor, and symbolism, as was the case with Pița's *Noiembrie, ultimul bal* (The Last Ball in November; 1989).[7]

The Party had no reason to fear such films, however. Audiences stood in line to see nationalist renderings of Western-inspired heroes of nineteenth-century Romania, situational comedies, and romances, all of which were soaked in socialist propaganda ("Situația numărului de spectatori"). Many Romanians lived "within a lie" and identified with the idealized characters on screen, thereby vicariously enjoying some sense of control over an otherwise increasingly taxing reality.[8] In a way, they saw their lives on screen: like the protagonists, they had come from humble origins, had confronted difficulties upon moving to the cities, but had persevered. What pushed some into the streets in 1989 was not necessarily a belief in a different value system, but the failure of the regime to provide for a reasonably comfortable life in the cities. The resistance to radical reforms that characterized Romania in the 1990s was not only a product of the former communist elites, but also the expression of a much broader appreciation for the welfare, paternalistic pre-1989 state.

The surprisingly swift fall of communism in Europe was, as historians have noted, the result of an economic crisis—the socialist states were no longer able to pay their increasing debt—and of the different regimes' willingness for "round table" meetings with the opposition within the civil society or the reforming factions within the communist parties (Kotkin 3–67; Ash, "Eastern Europe"). These changes were spurred, in most cases, by the population's desire for what was perceived to be the normal, modern life of Western Europe and by their expressed need to "return to Europe," the home of which they felt deprived for too long (Judt 630; Ash, "Eastern Europe"). Most socialist countries bridged the divide at the negotiating table, where they arrived after, sometimes, years of dialogue, as was the case with Poland and Hungary.

Romania was, again, different. It lacked both a visible civil society and a strong reforming wing within the Communist Party (Boia, *De ce e România altfel?* 109; Deletant 199–206). Important institutions that had contributed to the political change in other countries, such as the church or trade unions, were either silent and in cahoots with the regime, or nonexistent. The December 1989 uprising was triggered by a seemingly inconsequential event in Timişoara, a city in the western part of the country: A Hungarian-Romanian priest of the Reformed Church was forcefully removed from his parish by the Securitate (the Romanian Secret Police) (Deletant 232–40). Grapevine rumors, as well as broadcasts by international media outposts such as Radio Free Europe, Voice of America, BBC, or Deutsche Welle reached the millions isolated within their houses. Long-suppressed frustration, news of the fall of the Iron Curtain, and the promise of a decent life, free of humiliation, pushed many into the streets. Irrationally convinced that the population supported him, Ceauşescu addressed the masses he had ordered at a rally on December 21, 1989. The pre-recorded applause for his speech was drowned out by booing and shouting. "Command communication from the ruler to the people had broken down," comments, drily, the feminine voice in Harun Farocki and Andrei Ujică's *Videogramme einer Revolution* (Videograms of a Revolution; 1992) about this moment. Indeed, the "children" had finally turned against the Father. The images of Ceauşescu's execution had the effect of an earthquake.

Cristi Puiu was twenty-two years old in 1989. He had aspired to be a painter, but, as a young boy, he had failed the entrance exam into the Bucharest art school and had been assigned to a vocational high school. He found the classes boring and, alienated, preferred spending his time reading at home. It took him seven years to graduate. By December 1989, Puiu had been drafted into the army, and only chance prevented him from being sent into the streets, against the demonstrators.

Televised images were crucial to the new regime's rise to power. Historians now agree that the street revolt was doubled by a *coup d'état*, as groups within the Communist Party, the army, and the Securitate fought to gain supremacy (Constantinescu 441–50; Deletant 251–52; Tismaneanu 275–76; Judt 625). The live broadcast combined horrifying reports about imminent dangers to the population, with direct orders to the army and the Securitate, as new power structures and institutions were being established. The studio became the origin of the new world, and the birthing process appeared authentic and painful. It was at once a simulacrum and a real event (Baudrillard 56). For many, the apparent transparency of the medium and their own enthusiasm for a change legitimized what they saw, confirming their worst nightmares about the system. The communist edifice seemed to come down spectacularly, but the blood tribute it demanded shocked everybody. For the select few who could see, it was not a "demolition," but merely the application of a new "coat of paint": "democracy."

The spell of collective, synchronized emotion dissipated at the beginning of the 1990s, when the new power holders proved to be none other than the second and third tiers of the ex-Communist Party (Tismaneanu 286). Their initial orientation was not an attempt to "return to Europe," as was the case for their Central European counterparts, but rather a turn toward a new form of socialism. Ion Iliescu, the de-facto president, opted for what he infamously called an "original democracy," which kept the power in the hands of one party while masquerading as a multiparty system (Boia, *De ce e România altfel?* 112; Boia, *Romania* 148). With few exceptions, the feudalized public sphere continued to be the loudspeaker for the establishment, burying the new potentates' duplicitous behavior under a revived, often virulent, nationalistic discourse (Tismaneanu 291; Verdery 86–91).

Opposition to this neo-communist state was feeble, but radical. The 1989 revolutionaries in Timişoara drafted a proclamation renowned for its "Proposition #8," which required the political lustration of all those with important positions in the former Communist Party and the Securitate (Tismaneanu 284–85). Though never implemented, it was a sore spot for the state party still in power.

Political reorganization undermined economic stability. By April 1990, inflation and unemployment had risen rapidly, and many looked with fear toward an insecure future. There was a clear split between the working classes, who wanted to believe in the official, appeasing discourse, and the newly born civil society that felt betrayed. The split was also generational, with younger people largely opposing the new regime. In April 1990, one of the revived historical parties, the Christian-Democrat National Peasants' Party (CDNPP), organized a march in Bucharest, calling for a fair media representation of the opposition. The CDNPP had been declared illegal by the communists in 1947, and only a handful of its leaders had survived the many years of political imprisonment they had suffered. Puiu enrolled in this party almost immediately after its reestablishment in 1990. He would also join the many students and representatives of the intellectual classes who gathered in the University Square to demand that Proposition #8 be adopted before the first elections in May 1990.

The 1990 election, however, would prove a major gain for Iliescu's party. Ceaușescu's death had left empty the "father of the nation" pedestal he had so methodically constructed for decades; Iliescu's polite manners, soft voice, and calm demeanor made him the preferred benign father figure in the collective imaginary. This new "father," however, was not what he seemed. The University Square protest had already started to fizzle out when, on June 13, Iliescu called in the police, followed by groups of miners, to reestablish "order" and remove the "hooligans" (Boia, *România*, 152; Bohlen 2). The miners brutally attacked the protestors. Chance would, again, spare Puiu. In June 1990, he was in Lausanne, participating in an exhibition with six other Romanian artists. June 13–15, 1990 would remain in the public consciousness as the moment when the spirit of the 1989 change was surgically removed from the public sphere by the returning communist "father," in different attire. Part of an international constellation that includes the Tahrir, Taksim, or Maidan Squares, to name but a few, University Square continues to function as a space of open dissent to this day, being aligned, in people's memory, with an idealized search for truth, honor, and justice. Many of those attacked in 1990 had been out in the streets in December 1989. Their generation, ironically the "product" of Ceaușescu's 1966 antiabortion, would also give birth to the NRC.

The early 1990s were years of rapid enrichment for some, and of despair for many, as the gradual loss of social protection, the rise of xenophobia, and the constant weakening of the state at the hands of opportunistic "clans" left them with little hope for the future (Verdery 209–15). Companies were slowly privatized, often at the expense of the state, which was driven into insolvency by its ex-communist *nomenklatura*. This "buying out" process, through which the old establishment exchanged political for economic domination, was not unique to Romania, but it was particularly steeped in corruption in Bucharest (Ash, "Ten Years After"; Tismaneanu 295). The former apparatchiks lavishly displayed their overnight fortunes, while the victims of the communist regime and of the 1990s were consistently marginalized.[9] Emigration was the immediate escape; it reached a peak of 30,000 to 100,000 individuals per year between 1990 and 1993. An average of 20,000 people, mostly young, left Romania annually for the rest of the decade (Suciu 10).

The first change of regime was in 1996, when Emil Constantinescu, and a right-wing coalition of the revived historical parties and civic organizations, won the elections by a small margin (Boia, *România* 157). People's hopes were very high, especially because the new leader promised a moral reckoning with the past at a time when there was a widespread awareness of the deep involvement of the ex-Securitate officers in politics (Tismaneanu 290; Perlez). Internationally, Romania was, for the first time, recognized as an emerging democracy and, by the end of the decade, it was invited to become part of the EU (Boia, *România* 161). Reforms followed, but not at the pace many expected. Though important foreign investors finally arrived in Romania, the sense that the system continued to be corrupt lingered (Boia, *România* 158–60; Tismaneanu 281–82). The failure to confront and deal with the abuses of the communist period only further alienated the supporters of Constantinescu's regime. The end of the 1990s would find much of the population (up to 40 percent) living under the poverty threshold (Radu 90). Many looked back, with amnesiac reverence, to the social safety net of communism. The once politically silenced fathers had now become economically silenced as well; by 2000 their children had left the country in droves. Iliescu returned to power in 2000, as the "father" most people still preferred.

The political and economic turbulence of the 1990s was the direct result of a fierce confrontation between those ready to embrace Western values and those who regretted the passing of communism and its safeties. The dispute between these two groups also defined cultural life after 1989, particularly the transformations suffered by the film industry. The major instrument of communist inertia was the National Center for Cinematography (henceforth NCC or the Center), the very institution intended to reorganize Romanian cinema. Established in February 1990, it included the former managers of all state-owned film companies and had a threefold mission: to promote production, to ensure its high quality, and to take charge of the national film patrimony (Decret-Lege nr. 80). The Center was the only institution that could submit proposals to the government, which, in turn, provided the funds. Not surprisingly directors with privileges under the totalitarian regime continued to enjoy good access to state support in the 1990s.

One immediate reason for the persistence of the "old guard" is the network of connections, money, and power to which they belonged. Reform was only a matter of rebranding rather than structural and moral renewal. The existing five state studios were renamed, but continued to produce films for their former "clients" (Căliman 536). Regrouped into one giant company (Cinerom) in 1991 and privatized in 1996 as a new entity (Rofilm), these vestiges of communist management and practices would extend their influence well into the 2000s (Căliman 536; Uricaru 432). Rofilm would become infamous for its botched production of Puiu's first feature *Stuff and Dough*. To counterbalance the influence of the old establishment, director Lucian Pintilie petitioned the Ministry of Culture in 1991 and set up a parallel organization, the Film Studio of the Ministry of Culture (Studioul de creație cinematografică al Ministerului Culturii) (Uricaru 436). The lingering of the communist system in disguise revealed the sheer opportunism of its former supporters, who were more than eager to change sides to preserve their advantages.

The endurance of the "old guard" was equally a function of newcomers' difficulty in making their debut. In the 1990s, the National University of Theater and Film "I. L. Caragiale" was the only important institution training the new generations of cinema professionals. With few exceptions, their professors remained the same before and after 1989; therefore, many of the upcoming filmmakers were stylistically indebted to them. Economically, the new generation also depended on the endorsement of the old one in order to have access to state funding. After 1990, a year when no new productions were released, 1991 and

1992 welcomed eight new filmmakers, of whom only one would still be working by 2000 (Căliman 508, 523–34). Only two of the new films were made with private funding (Căliman 527). By 1994, the number of short films, the most accessible form of artistic expression for young directors, decreased rapidly in the absence of a coherent cultural policy (Căliman 592).

Another factor that severely undermined the rise of a new generation was the increasing poverty of the film industry. The 123 percent drop in the value of the Romanian currency in 1997 and the crashing of the banking system by 2000 almost depleted the state's reserves for nonprofit economic sectors (Radu 20). Although the National Cinema Fund was established in 1997 to ward off dangers, the state's financial investment in cinema had dropped so much by that time that in 2000, as in 1990, no films were produced (Radu 141; Uricaru 433; M. Dumitrescu 86).

At the same time, the price of film tickets rose dramatically, overtaking, by 60 to 80 percent, the price of tickets in the EU (when related to the value of the average salary) (Radu 138). If 130 million cinema tickets were sold in 1990, by 1999 they totaled only 40 million (Radu 139). In the absence of any significant investment in the existing exhibition venues, and as new laws regarding privatization allowed the NCC to rent out and sell cinema theaters, the 595 cinemas in use in 1990 were reduced to only 270 by 2000 (Radu 140). The situation was made even worse by the chaotic, unrestrained import, especially of American films; by 1997, 532 out of a total of 821 imported films were made in the United States (M. Dumitrescu 86). The advent of cable television and of the rental store only aggravated matters. In one decade, Romanian cinema faced all the challenges posed to its European counterpart in the previous thirty years. If the top-grossing Romanian film of 1992, *Liceenii rock'n'roll* (High School Rock 'n' Roll), a romantic comedy, yielded $ 2.87 million in sales, *Triunghiul morții* (The Death Triangle), a nationalist historical, drama made only $34,370 in 1999 (Radu 150–51). The local cinema had lost its viewers.

State funding for cinema was dwindling across Europe in the 1990s. By 1994, more than half of the necessary funds came from private enterprises, especially television channels (Galt 103). In Romania, the state television did help a few established directors and even new filmmakers such as Radu Muntean, but its support remained very low compared to the necessity (Căliman 604). A few European companies invested in films by Romanian directors (such as Nae Caranfil and Radu Mihăileanu), but the most significant involvement was that of the EURIMAGES program, established in 1989 in order to foster coproductions (Pricop 96). Romania joined this program in 1998; in 2000, Nae Caranfil would receive funding for *Philanthropy* (*Filantropica*; 2000), followed by NRC directors such as Călin Peter Netzer in 2001, Alexandru Solomon in 2003, and Cătălin Mitulescu in 2005 ("EURIMAGES").

A different type of support for the recent film school graduates would come from other foreign investments. Castel Films, established in collaboration with Paramount, and the MediaPro European consortium launched into the large-scale production of B-rated movies, and soon upgraded to box-office hits such as *Cold Mountain* (2002), *Callas Forever* (2002), and *Amen* (2002) (Uricaru 440; Căliman 535–36). NRC filmmakers Radu Jude and Adrian Sitaru started their careers working as assistant directors for such large-scale productions.

This evolution, however, was not easily predictable in the 1990s, during the race for state money and studios. Cinema became merely craftsmanship: Directors delivered standard products in standard time. The only difference between the standardized products of the 1980s and those of the 1990s was in their ideological reorientation: Now the communists were to blame for the nation's decay, as had once been the case with the capitalistic bourgeois or the corrupted intellectual.

Excess, desperation, and a rush to rewrite history dominated 1990s cinema. Given the freedom to approach any subject, directors obsessively attempted to reconfigure the past and the events of 1989. Nationalistic propaganda about exceptional individuals dominated the bill, from the contested figure of Marshal Ion Antonescu, to those of World War II fighters and anticommunist resistance heroes.[10] History, even when "refurbished" with denunciations of communist atrocities, was merely the pretext for an inflated portrait of the nation and, possibly, a source of reassurance for the befuddled postcommunist subject. Puiu would flatly reject this new nationalist propaganda.

The almost neurotic return to the 1940s was not unique for Romanian cinema, however. Rosalind Galt has observed that, in the 1990s, films targeting that decade were part of a larger, European redefinition of new, post–Iron Curtain identities (108–10). Unlike their European counterparts, the Romanian historical films generated very limited debates about the ethics behind their reconstruction of the past (Galt 108–10). Romanian critics such as Valerian Sava and Alex. Leo Șerban attacked them for their flimsy scriptwriting and extravagant costs, or critiqued their easy surrender to a consumerist philosophy: they were the "dreams" the masses desired (Sava, "Falimentul cinematografiei buftene"; Șerban, *De ce vedem filme* 40–43). With few exceptions, these films were made by directors who had, if not served the communist regime, then, at least, collaborated and profited from it, hence their morally questionable nature.

The question of moral guilt became more poignant in films addressing the 1989 events and their aftermath, many of which were the work of former dissident directors. They evoked a world in dissolution, with grotesque characters, decaying institutions, and traumatized victims.[11] Hopeless and confused, ordinary people were dragged into conflicts they could neither understand nor escape unharmed. Overt sexual acts and graphic violence abounded. Romanian critic Angelo Mitchievici argues that total freedom of expression encouraged filmmakers to "'scream' out what [was] evident" (50).

In a sense, these films were a gut response to years of "traumatic citizenship." The "scream," however, was not one of liberation, but of frustration and impotence. Writing about the challenges facing post-1945 Germany, Karl Jaspers emphasized the need for an "ethical self-examination" and the search for truth in the absence of loud sentiment that could only bog it down (12–14, 25). In Romanian cinema, loud sentiment took the stage and, eventually, alienated audiences. Puiu and the NRC would reject the "scream." Furthermore, the task of working through the past was very much complicated not only by commercial considerations inherent in a nascent market economy, but also by the absence of moral restitution to the victims. In fiction cinema, the investigation into what represented historical reality and the means through which such reality was constituted would become essential to the NRC.

A more honest, yet not unproblematic, attempt at examining the past was undertaken by the documentary. More than sixty-five films were made in 1990 alone, many of which focused on the December uprising and the enduring effects of the communist era (Căliman 515–17). Probably the best known of these, Gulea's *Piața Universității—Romania*

(University Square—Romania; 1991) chronicled the 1990 opposition to Iliescu's regime, giving voice to the discontent of the intellectual classes in the aftermath of the miners' attack. The number of such films dropped dramatically throughout the 1990s, and by the end of the decade, they remained almost exclusively the prerogative of the national television (Căliman 582–84). Among them, Lucia Hossu-Longin's *Memorialul durerii* (The Chronicles of Pain; 1991–1997) has achieved the status of a *lieu de memoire* itself. A TV series including more than 150,000 minutes of interviews, confessions, documents, archival images, and reenactments, *The Chronicles* adopted some of the methods of investigation pioneered by Claude Lanzmann in *Shoah* (1985), as Hossu-Longin herself traveled to many of the former communist prisons and uncovered important documents about the victims and their executioners (Gurescu). The series preserved a grave, somber tone throughout, steering away from easy didacticism or loud accusation. The question of memory, moral reckoning with the past, and the fate of the individual at the mercy of history would return in full force in the NRC.

1990s audiences, however, were more interested in the pleasures promised by the present. Among these, sexual liberation toppled everything else. The most commercially successful film of the decade was Nicolae Corjos's *High School Rock 'n' Roll,* the sequel to the very popular *Liceenii* (The Graduates; 1986), in which teenagers fight prejudice and fall in love under the strict surveillance of their teachers, parents, and . . . the Party. The 1992 version undressed the protagonists in, now, overt lovemaking scenes, gathering more than 2.8 million viewers (Radu 150). Mircea Mureșan's *Miss Litoral* (1990) and *A doua cădere a Constantinopolului* (The Second Fall of Constantinople; 1994) each sold more than 1.3 million tickets, ranking second and third in terms of number of viewers for the decade (Radu 150). More a pretext for nudity and slapstick than real narratives, these two comedies were devoid of references to the past and turned the difficulties of the present into an occasion for laughter and vulgarity. Romanian critics have categorized such films as "gutter cinema," but one may as well consider them triggers for scopophilia as a form of psychological release (Sava, *O istorie,* vol. 1: 23). They were the only ones to withstand the onslaught of American blockbusters.

One remarkable continuity between the 1980s and the 1990s cinema needs mentioning: its lackluster aesthetics. Most films relied on classical Hollywood editing, which they combined with on-location shooting and a preference for extraordinary characters. The more stylistically aware directors paid close attention to *mise en scène* and camera movement, often relying on visual symbolism for more depth. In time, however, such methods became overly didactic clichés, as if intended for an audience that constantly needed to be poked in order to "follow" the message. Even when anchored in contemporary realities, films functioned according to long-established conventions, and nothing was more artificial than the language, gestures, and tones of the characters. They spoke in a literary fashion and cursed in full, complex sentences. Most were only "painted dolls," to borrow Juan Antonio Bardem's term: empty inside, yet expressing outward emotions.[12]

By the end of the 1990s, Romanian cinema was falling into a rut. It had exhausted itself in nationalistic charades, moral indictments, sexual fantasies, and violent rages. It still "talked" in the obsolete, lifeless visual language of the 1980s. Most importantly, it failed to break convention and remained isolated in its own bubble. In a society of corrupt or powerless fathers, the need to reevaluate the past, to question memory and memory-making, and to establish new principles of representation became even more acute. Cristi Puiu would be the first to use cinema as an instrument for the investigation of the past. He would also be the most radical.

Theater of Memory: *The Retirement Home*

The 1990s were formative years for Puiu, whose restlessness and rebelliousness constantly pushed him onto paths not lightly trodden. After the 1990 Lausanne exhibition, he returned to Romania, where he moved from one job to the next and pursued his interest in art. In 1992, he was accepted into the École Supérieure d'Arts Visuels in Geneva to study painting. After a year, however, he changed his major to filmmaking, and did not look back.

Upon graduation in 1996, Puiu returned home, where he was a stranger to the state film producers, the film school, and the critics, but, more importantly, to the type of under-the-counter arrangements that dominated public affairs. He started working for a private television channel and, in 1998, when fellow director Andreea Păduraru suggested that they should make a documentary, Puiu joined the project. The setting was one of the few remaining senior living facilities in Romania, situated in Craiova, a city in the southwest of the country. This fortuitous experience became an opportunity to reflect on old age, the decaying body, and death. It would mark Puiu for many years to come, eventually pushing him to write and direct his breakthrough film *Mr. Lazarescu*.

The Retirement Home is a first-person narrative about the workings of an institution, following in the footsteps of Frederick Wiseman and Raymond Depardon. It combines an interest in social issues with a contemplative look at the elderly and the nurses, doctors, and administrative personnel with whom they share their lives. There is no drama, no loud indictments, and no "voice of God." Quite the contrary, the young woman engaged in dialogue with the various "characters" (Andreea Păduraru) and the accompanying camera seem curious and genuinely interested in people's stories. The film includes emotional interviews, moments of performance, and, at times, the air of an out-of-date educational video cranked out at random by an unseen communist ghost whom the nurses and the patients freely acknowledge. Păduraru and Puiu's participatory documentary is more the work of cultural anthropologists exploring a new, unfamiliar community than that of script-based filmmakers.[13] They pay such constant attention to the spaces—both outer and inner—through which they, and their "protagonists," travel, that *The Retirement Home* becomes an emotional journey through an unexpected history, much different from the one superficially denounced in the media.

Working through the past, Păduraru and Puiu suggest, requires neither the histrionic "scream" of frustration and revolt of the 1990s Romanian cinema, nor the cold, clinical gaze of observational cinema, but a lucid, compassionate relationship with the places that have recorded it and the people who have lived it. *The Retirement Home* relies on image hapticity and the detailed depiction of human solidarity within the institution in order to stimulate viewers' affective engagement with its subjects. Individual nostalgia for an otherwise confusing, contested collective past eventually takes over the narrative, as spectators are invited to ponder the ways in which the film itself shapes and preserves memory.

The codirectors' journey starts with a photomontage of the various streets through which their car approaches the "filming" site: a square with a church and a few post-1989 deli kiosks, a creaky old bus, a narrow curve in between two early 1900s houses, more houses and trees, a boulevard and its few imposing buildings whose social-realist architecture dates this part of the city to the 1960s, and, finally, a green, metallic gate. The city is a mishmash of styles and periods, as different constructions, mostly residential, pop out or hide behind the rather luxuriant canopy of trees. Streets are populated by old trucks and buses, and by the occasional old Dacia, the national automobile brand. With the exception of the mushrooming kiosks—tokens of incipient capitalist initiative—there is little to indicate that the communist regime has expired. In fact, the general impression is of a place frozen in time, in which ivy-covered houses endure side by side with the once arrogant, bulky edifices, and the brash little stores of the new era. The off-screen commentary neutrally describes the road as the link between the peripheral location of the retirement community and the heart of the city; it further explains that the photos were taken very early on the morning of July 19, the last day of filming. The ensemble suggests a recurring movement: of the shooting crew between the site and the hotel in the city center; of the film narrative, between the last frame and this beginning; and, on a metaphorical level, of history itself, between its current remapping and the inheritance of bankrupt socialism. This is a journey, it is suggested, of memory and affect that return in waves; it is a search for a sense of shared experience and a path to self-reflection.

Space and memory are central to the film's argument. Organized as a palimpsest, the spaces we inhabit deposit history in their folds. Of them, Henri Lefebvre writes, "No space ever vanishes utterly, leaving no trace. Even the sites of Troy, Susa, or Leptis Magna still enshrine the superimposed spaces of the succession of cities that have occupied them" (164). More than the physical traces of previous cities, the ever-evolving streets and buildings are imbued with the symbols, values, images, that is, with the "lived experience" of generations of dwellers (Lefebvre 39). The retirement home is such a space: isolated and forgotten, it shelters the emotional histories of the discarded. Păduraru and Puiu's documentary excavates and dusts them for its viewers.

Space soaked into emotion is also at the center of Giuliana Bruno's *Atlas of Emotion*. She argues that urban geography has often been the site of personal emotion, distinctly evoked in modern writing as early as 1654 (2, 258–59). Physical journeys through gardens and streets trigger inner ones, through bodily recollection and imagination. Moreover, visual representations of space can, sometimes, have similar effects, as images stimulate not only the eye, but also one's tactile and kinesthetic senses, thereby "moving" viewers' affection (Bruno 6, 250–54). The "haptic," evocative quality of the image converts film into the keeper and producer of cultural memory (Bruno 7). Bruno develops an idea expressed earlier by Annette Michaelson in her analysis of the haptic rendering of movement in space in Stanley Kubrick's *2001: A Space Odyssey* (1968), "Viewing becomes the discovery, through the acknowledgment of disorientation, of what it is to see, to learn, to know, and of what it is to be, seeing" (56). I suggest, therefore, that in Păduraru and Puiu's film, hapticity is an epistemological instrument that infuses one's sharp intellectual examination of the image with the warmth of recollected emotion.

The Retirement Home relies on haptic reproductions of spaces, objects, and bodies to depict a vanishing world. The peeling paint on walls and furniture, the rusty machines in the laundromat and the kitchen, and the creaking sounds of food carts reach beyond the screen, as atemporal signifiers of bodily decay in perfect symbiosis with the men and women they still serve. The result is a meditation on the ways in which History intersects, determines, and washes away the private histories of anonymous individuals. Hapticity thus establishes viewers' affective relationship with the observed subject (as it would also do in Puiu's later films, especially in *Mr. Lazarescu*).

The documentary appears to be the x-ray of an institution. Several chapters examine every aspect of life within: the management; the laundromat; the doctor's visits; food supply; cooking; lunch; pension day; and memories. Each chapter is preceded by a prologue, often, but not always, in the form of a montage of photos accompanied by a bland, voiceover statement of facts. Eventually, the film abandons its rather rational organization in favor of a more fluid development of life moments, as engagement with the various individuals carries the directors from one story to another and back; affect replaces the clinical observation of facts. Păduraru and Puiu are unavoidably invited into a more personal, emotional relationship with the people they meet, all of whom appear quite eager to help them and await their directions; this will be the impression that most lingers with viewers after the film credits have rolled. Information is purposely fragmented, whether in the form of the recurring photos that stop the flow of camera time, or by means of abruptly introducing interviews or cutting them short ahead of time, in the latter part of the narrative. There is a constant sense that something is missing and that full details are simply impossible to obtain.

Not that information is completely refused; quite the contrary, viewers are presented with very clear statistics about the Home. One finds out that 330 employees are in charge of 475 patients; that the cost of care is about $37 per month, which is often more than their pensions can afford (the difference is paid from the state budget); and that the Home receives about 500 loaves of bread per day. The photos tell a richer story. At the beginning, the medium long shot of a building foyer reveals four empty chairs and a dial phone posted so high up on the wall that one wonders how anybody could use it. This waiting room is a visual metonymy for the entire Home; it is a space where the old, the sick, and the abandoned come to "wait" for their time to cross over. Peeling paint and a rusted half pipe suggest that the radiator once nested against the wall has been replaced by the row of chairs. This is a banal and absurd space, whose functionality is evident, yet questionable. Who are the people who sit on these chairs? When do they do so and why? Who has used the phone? Why was this space turned into a waiting room? The impression of life eroded in time is conveyed, throughout the film, by means of various graphic matches: the peeling wall matches the peeling paint on the rack of bread loaves, in another photo, or on the bread truck and the shoddy metal night tables in the patients' rooms, in further sequences; they all eventually converge in the memorable image of the human body "peeling" away, memory by memory, and, then, skin layer by skin layer, in the last scene. Hapticity becomes, thus, an occasion for viewers' direct, carnal knowledge of the corrosiveness of time and the vulnerability of the human body. In its imagery, *The Retirement Home* indirectly muses on the fate of the many little facts, sensations, events,

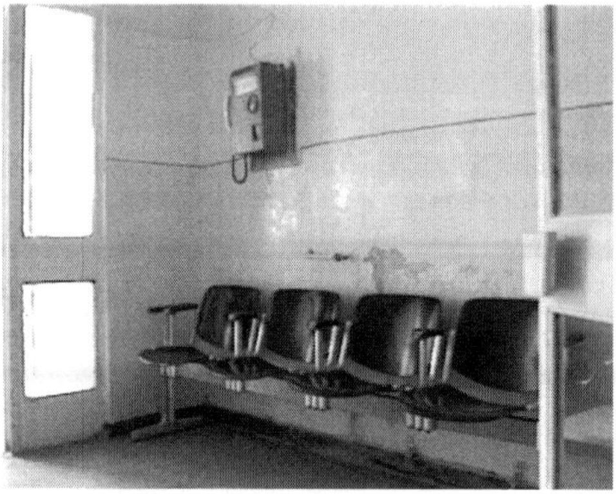

Figure 1: The Waiting Room

and memories that make up one's lived experience at the end of a life journey. How much is left behind, as part of a larger, communal experience passed on to the new occupants of the chairs in the foyer?

At the very heart of the film lies the metaphor of time as a giant washing machine, so it is not by chance that the first activity depicted is that of doing laundry. Nurses methodically pull out old linens, stuff them into white cloth bags, and replace them with clean, even if ragged, sheets. The bags are carried to a huge room, where they are thrown into the belly of a behemoth, a 1950s industrial washing machine. Taller and much larger than a human being, this contraption is fascinating in its mechanism: two women are needed to close the latches of its first door, and slide a second trapdoor over it. Two bars are pulled with a strong arm, then a few buttons are switched on; the sounds of water and the turning drum invade the whole room. The camera pans over four old dryers, then back to the washing machine as the caretaker opens its belly to let the water run down a drain in the floor. A gripping, medium shot image of the spewing beast ends this sequence: layers of paint have been peeling off, as rust and a white, powdery substance have taken over. Water leaks out even after the laundress closes the monster's belly door shut.

The whole process is a visual representation of a much larger, historical evolution. At an immediate level, it is symptomatic of the transition between two regimes, when old slogans, fears, even people were

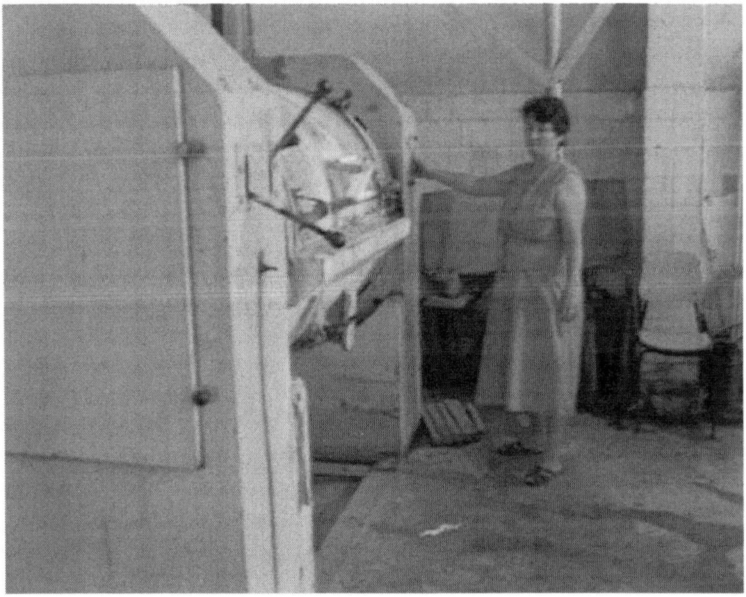

Figure 2: Chronos |

recycled to fit the new times. The machine also stands in for the wheels of History swallowing and soaking individuals in its ideology only to wring them dry for a new "wear" when triggered from without. The most vulnerable are the abject and the forgotten, who reside, as the patients of this Home do, at the periphery of social and economic life. At a deeper level, the machine reminds one of Chronos devouring its children. References to mortality and the closeness of death abound in the documentary, from the rather long poem performed by one of the patients (in which a newlywed bride drowns together with the whole wedding party) to the slew of dead relatives in the photos of another.

More spectacularly, the film pays close attention to the decaying human body in its last sequence where, again, washing becomes a ritual that seems to prepare the man for an imminent crossing of the Styx. Coiled in the fetal position, Mr. Popescu is tenderly cared for by both the nurse and the camera. As the woman pours water from a few bottles onto the bed linen and uses them to wipe clean his skin, the camera preserves a medium-length distance from the protagonists, close enough to reveal the creases in the body, the ulcerations and mild infections that have taken over parts of it, yet sufficiently far to preserve the man's identity and emphasize his frailty. Viewers may experience a carnal sensation of skin peeling away with the wet cloth, a sensation that invites their reflection on their own mortality.

Haptic imagery, however, is not the only trigger for viewers' emotional engagement with the observed subjects. The solidarity established within the institution, revealed in the least scripted moments of the film, is also emotionally stirring. The warmhearted collaboration between Mr. Popescu and his nurse percolates beyond the screen. She tenderly calls him "Pops," and does not shy away from touching and rubbing his body with the affection that has grown from their long-time connection. Their interaction highlights the importance of the little gestures comforting one in need, as well as the transience of the human condition.

One outlasting impression is that, short of proper supplies, equipment, and adequate work conditions, the staff do their utmost to help patients. Good intentions and the desire to protect the elderly prevail at each hierarchical level. The Home's manager is a young, rather shy woman who constantly averts her eyes from the camera. She explains the institution's dependence on funding from a national agency, while the piles of folders on her desk are visual reminders of the bureaucratic quagmires she must address. They talk of the absence of deep reforms in a system that has all but abandoned its most vulnerable citizens. The buildings these old men and women inhabit, the beds they sleep in, and even the metal bowls they use have all probably been part of the inventory at least since the 1970s. More than a transition between two opposite regimes, the film suggests, the 1990s witnessed their prolonged interdependence.

Doctors further supervise the life of the institution, but their relationship with the patients is even more personal. The camera follows a mild-mannered woman in her forties on her morning rounds. She chats with her patients and comforts them about their ailments with motherly tenderness and attention. By contrast, the nurses have adopted the position of their "(grand)daughters," often referring to them by endearing words such as "dad," "pops," or "grandpa." Their work is one of filial duty, which allows the elderly to preserve their dignity and gives them a measure of self-worth that the outside society has denied them. The general impression, therefore, is that this decrepit institution is, indeed, a "home," sheltering not patients but an extended family, probably among the most functional in the NRC.

The same solidarity with the other as an incentive for self-analysis transpires from the camera's relationship with its "subjects." Handheld and endowed with a palpable presence, this guest observer becomes an interlocutor acknowledged as such by everybody in the Home. Its appearance in a room prompts most, though not all, "characters" into self-conscious performance. Such is the case with the cook's long exposition of her daily chores. The kitchen where she works is narrow, poorly lit, and stacked with old ovens and stoves, but she never complains about anything. Huge pots of soups, stews, and dessert lie in waiting on a long metal table, and, as the camera pans over them, the tiled walls behind reveal exposed pipes, cracks, improper sealing, and accumulated stains. The "star" of the kitchen is the "robot" used to mix cake dough or mash potatoes. It is a heavy, metal machine, once white, now covered in rust; the cook rapidly wipes off a little flour dust, glancing furtively at the camera, as if that were the only problem in the whole "setting."

There is a marked contrast between the ancient furniture and appliances in this kitchen and the woman's undauntedness in front of the camera. She readily and, at times, with pride, explains each process, pointing with her hands at each pot; her stiff gestures and ceremonious words belong in one of the communist educational videos of the past. 1998 was still a few good years away from the digital revolution, but the cook's deference to the camera is that of a society in which moving images were always the instruments of official surveillance (and, therefore, a matter of make-believe). Her performance—rigid, but endearing—is, in a way, on a par with that of the shy manager, or that of the caretakers, who call their friends, very formally, "laundry ladies." Păduraru and Puiu's curious, unscripted camera, and their young ages at the time, probably confused many of the employees, and it is especially funny when they try to "help" the film "students." The women's warmth and understanding toward the directors, unlike their performance for the camera, is genuine and unmediated. It transcends the screen, inviting viewers to ponder on the value of kindness among relative strangers, especially poignant in a growingly fragmented society

Another means through which the film engages viewers in an affective examination of the observed world is by undermining their expectations about the men and women on screen. In spite of its overall somber mood, *The Retirement Home* is also a celebration of human endurance. Mr. Nedelcu, one of the patients, makes regular trips to the little farmers' market near the Home, where vendors have spilled out of the designated area and, under a few colorful umbrellas, have spread their produce on makeshift tables on the sidewalk. An old electrical post, serving as support for circulation signs and smaller ads, is tilted and, like the rest of the scene, slightly "out of order." Life bursts out at the seams, in spite of the relative precariousness of the space. Mr. Nedelcu embraces it: he buys coffee, condiments, and chocolate for the grandchildren who may come to visit. He even buys two lottery tickets in what appears to be a recurring ritual. Alone, sick, and financially challenged, this man has not given up; he is as much alive as the street bustle he joins.

So is Mr. Alexandru, one of the most colorful "characters" in the documentary. He is an artist with a penchant for singing and improvising, and the filming crew possibly provides an incentive for his performance. In a memorable sequence, he uses a broomstick as "guitar" and, facing the camera, but with his back turned to his regular "audience," he recites a long poem about the drowning of an entire wedding party. There is dark humor in his "story," and, though tragic, it entertains his spectators. A cut to a long shot reveals several men and women who, probably, spend their afternoons chatting with each other and listening to him. Like Mr. Alexandru and Mr. Nedelcu, they have found the little "nothings" to fill their time. Though mostly confined, the lives of the forsaken others appear richer than one may imagine.

The impression of bustling inner life is also the "product" of the last section of the film titled "Fragments." The attention paid to memory and storytelling is a self-reflexive act that exposes the limitations of any narrative to depict the fullness of life. Filmed with a fixed camera, placed close to the "subjects," the final segment includes interviews with a few patients, some of whom have already been "featured" in the film. In the prologue to this part, Păduraru and Mrs. Mihăilă are looking at the latter's family photos. In all sizes, these black-and-white artifacts are laid out on a table as the voluble woman zealously explains each of them: her mother on the death bed; the funeral of her husband; the sister who was accidentally shot dead; or the cousin who was hung. As more photos come into discussion, some revealed to the camera, others not, the fragmentary "story" of her life takes shape. Born in 1927, she was raised in a closely knit family, graduated only with a primary education, married a priest, and attended various relatives' weddings, funerals, and other events. She describes some of them with accuracy; others she barely mentions. She claims to be lucky to remember everything, but, toward the end, she misremembers the name of close friends (which Păduraru reads on the back of the photo). This small detail throws her entire "story" into question and exposes the role memory plays in constantly reshaping one's identity. How much is true of what she says? How much is misinterpreted? How much has been forgotten and how much did she want to forget? The family photo album is a site of constant return, profoundly impregnated by emotions, and always wrapped in a nostalgic aura. It opens, as Marianne Hirsch suggests, a space "between the myth of the ideal family and the lived reality of family life," a space impregnated by absence and loss, and compulsively reinvented in narratives that only reinforce its ultimate unavailability (8, 23). Film, the

Figure 3: Photo narrative |

directors suggest, functions in a similar way: it truncates information, rearranges it, and delivers it as an apparently coherent discourse. It pushes the past further away. The "fragments" of interviews that follow are to be interpreted with the care and tenderness one grants old family photos.

"Which was the most beautiful day of your life?" asked the directors. Most of the answers focus, surprisingly, on speakers' dramas. A law graduate remembers being admitted into the Home in her early forties, marrying there, and being widowed the year before. Another discusses her discovery of her Jewish roots when the Russian and Romanian police came to arrest her family, probably in the late 1940s, early 1950s. A third recalls the tragic earthquake of 1977 and her son's death from cancer a few days later. A veteran remembers being held prisoner for more than a year in Russia toward the end of World War II. Mr. Nedelcu vividly describes the day when, as he was being transported between two villages he was observing as a state accountant, the driver of the horse-cart stopped to show him a valley where the communists had executed and buried many opponents. "People knew about it, but nobody had the guts to tell. They were afraid. And it was natural to be like this," he argues. The most "beautiful" days in their lives have been buried, like Mrs. Mihăilă's photos of marriages, deep under stories of loss, most of which date back to World War II and its aftermath. It is a return to a site of trauma that had been rewritten during communism, and that was, in the post-1989 decade, beginning to be recovered and redefined. It is also a sign of refusal to turn back to the immediate past, the forty years that followed 1947 and, thus, an effort to disremember it. Fear and the desire to protect one's family, says Mr. Nedelcu, can explain people's lack of resistance to the authorities. His sincere look at the past speaks of the difficulty of living split in two between the self that desires to return to one's youth with love, and the self that is publicly accused of historical cowardice and forbidden the return. It is Mr. Nedelcu's decent, humane relationship with the past that the film seeks to reproduce.

Three other interviews stand out for their incongruity. Mr. Mihalache, whom we meet as a patient earlier, talks about his love for his profession as a printer and his devotion to it. There is no mentioning of suffering or loss in his testimony. A woman with big glasses valiantly describes her confrontation with the former presidential pair, Elena and Nicolae Ceaușescu. Her story is absurd and funny, most probably an indication of her withdrawal into an inner imaginary life rather than a factual recollection. Also absurd and humorous, tinged by a Dadaist spirit, is Mr. Alexandru's final long poem about a few men preparing to go on a journey, but being diverted onto a dead-end track (an appropriate metaphor for life in communism). He remembers telling it to entertain his young wife when they came back tired from work. In their directly expressed or implied affection for the objectionable past as the locus of their youth, the patients of this last communist Home stand apart from the 1990s public discourse. For them, nostalgia is a more honest relationship with the past than simulated outrage, Păduraru and Puiu suggest. Through the camera's loving look, these storytellers, bedridden, abandoned, and lonely, are no longer the wounded wards of an indifferent state, but honorable members of the nation.

The Retirement Home could have easily been an indictment of the past and of a corrupted present society that has forgotten its elders in its rush for capital. Decrepit furniture, peeling walls, and antiquated machines would have provided immediate, and facile, evidence for serious charges against both regimes. Instead, it is a tender look at the affectionate relationships developed under less than ideal circumstances in one of the many derelict institutions of the past. In reenacting the meeting between the camera and the various dwellers and employees of the institution, the documentary itself becomes a cultural site of memory.

The Road Not Taken: *Stuff and Dough*

In *Stuff and Dough,* Puiu's empathetic look would focus on a different category of flawed human beings: the youth. The film represents, in a way, the director's reflection on the obstacles and dangers his own generation faced when pursuing otherwise unspectacular dreams. If *The Retirement Home* turns a tender eye to the "grandparents" (who had witnessed the brutal advent of communism), *Stuff and Dough* sets the stage for what would become an almost obsessive theme not only in Puiu's cinema, but also in the NRC: the relationship between fathers and sons.

The very making of this first feature in the late 1990s was undermined by the fathers' attempt to keep a son in line. Financed by the state, through the NCC, Puiu's film was produced by Rofilm, the ex-communist mammoth company, now under private patronage. *Stuff and Dough* caused serious disagreements between the company's representatives, who became increasingly unhappy with Puiu's type of cinema, and the director, who refused to make major compromises in his work ethic or aesthetic philosophy. Rofilm was accused of providing insufficient funding and incompetent management (Puiu, "Cineva trebuie"; Chirilov and Sandu 51–53). They threatened to prevent the film's screening in Cannes, where it had been selected for the Directors' Fortnight section (Sava, *O istorie,* vol. 1: 285). Eventually, they cut the postproduction funds, jeopardizing the project; the Film Studio, under Lucian Pintilie's patronage, saved it (Uricaru 436). When *Stuff and Dough* premiered on June 1, 2001, in Bucharest, the NCC and Rofilm did not send any representatives to support it. Very few copies were made for distribution and the film was forbidden to young people under eighteen (Sava, *O istorie,* vol. 1: 93). Only 1,963 viewers paid a ticket to watch it on the big screen in Romania (Sava, *O istorie,* vol. 1: 139).

Stuff and Dough bothered many of the old-time cinema officials because it was an absolute novelty to the local tradition and it was conceived by an unknown young director relentless in his vision of cinema as an instrument of exploration rather than storytelling. The film was deceptively simple in narrative form, apparently unpolished in style, and wrenchingly powerful in its actors' impact beyond the screen; more importantly, it proposed no closure to the moral dilemmas it raised. This was simply the road not taken by Romanian cinema.

The plot appears quite banal. Ovidiu (Alexandru Papadopol) is a young man in his twenties who lives a rather difficult life in Constanța, a city on the Black Sea coast where the other, more famous Ovid, author of the *Metamorphoses,* ended his life in exile. Puiu's choice of name is suggestive of the inner exile to which his protagonist would submit himself by the end of his journey. Ovidiu lives with his parents in a small apartment that also serves as a makeshift store for their neighbors. One morning, the protagonist is hastily awakened by Marcel Ivanov (Răzvan Rădulescu), a slick, macho-looking small-time businessman, who gives him a leather bag full of six packets of "medicines" for a certain Doncea (Doru Ana) in Bucharest. Although he is told not to take anybody with him, Ovidiu calls his buddy, Vali (Dragoș Bucur), who shows up with his new girl, Betty (Ioana Flora). The three have a quick coffee in the kitchen, where Ovidiu's mother, Caty (Luminița Gheorghiu) hands them a list of products they need to buy from a wholesale supermarket in Bucharest.

Most of the film is spent on the road, where the friends exchange opinions on everything that tickles their fancy: their dreams, music, the buildings they pass by, or the virtues of one car brand over another. Out of the blue, they are attacked by a red SUV, manage to escape, and after some delay, deliver the "stuff." On the way back, Ovidiu decides, on a whim, to take a shortcut only to come across the SUV, whose passengers have all been executed. Back home, Marcel is waiting for them. He hands Ovidiu the second half of his payment and enlists Vali as the driver for his next package. When the protagonist tries to back out, the now fully revealed dangerous mafia leader threatens to kill his entire family. The film ends with a pensive Ovidiu slowly chewing the french fries his work-exhausted mother has prepared for him. The paths one takes are often treacherous and may well lead deeper into the woods than out of them, as the protagonist realizes too late.

A road movie, *Stuff and Dough* subverts generic expectations and focuses on the inner, rather than outer, drama. Ovidiu and Vali have a

Figure 4: On the road |

specific goal to achieve—delivering the drugs—and, early on, it is clear that their trip is not without its perils. Suspense builds with every appearance and disappearance of the red SUV, especially because there is no explanation for what is happening. Regardless of how close a decisive confrontation may seem, it never occurs and the accumulating tension is never released. "If you get attacked, you get scared and then you don't think straight. You remember movies and imagine they're going to run you off the road," Ovidiu comments after they are ambushed. The film, thus, signals its own condition as fiction and highlights viewers' own cultivated assumptions of similar situations.

The script was written by two novices: Cristi Puiu and Răzvan Rădulescu. Having tried to publish his first novel three times and failed, Rădulescu perceived this project as a change of pace (Chirilov and Sandu 53).[14] For Puiu, the subject was very personal. After 1989, he often found himself in situations that pushed him to make compromises in order to put his ideas into practice. The film was triggered by his frustration with the "new" world, but was inspired by a more painful experience: In 1998, his wife's brother, a cybernetics graduate, died in a car crash as he was trying to expand his small commercial business (Chirilov and Sandu 54). These little, but daunting concessions that many young people had to make in the 1990s are discreetly condensed into the one compromise Ovidiu makes: the transport of a small quantity of drugs.

Many others were pushed into situations for which they were not prepared in the late 1990s and the early 2000s, a period marked by contradictory trends. The gradual consolidation of the EU, and the specter of instability haunting Romania from its eastern and southern borders, pulled politicians more firmly toward the West. The privatization of important economic sectors continued, and economic growth went up from 5 percent in 2000 to 8 percent in 2004, a spectacular rise in Eastern Europe at the time (Boia, *România* 172). Toward the end of the 1990s, consumption also accelerated, and small mom and pop stores, like the one Ovidiu's parents own, cropped up everywhere. For some, the 2000s would be the years of splurging, an expression of their desire to "live deeply, to feel existence" (Roman 54).

The counterbalance to this apparent prosperity was the dramatic deterioration of the social safety net. Hiding behind the banners of "free" market and "democracy" was a state that increasingly passed its responsibilities on to the individual. Privatization meant, in many cases, that large numbers of employees were laid off. The more fortunate found new jobs, some full-time, many part-time or temporary; even then, private, nonunionized companies required long hours and offered less employment security. Others ran through unemployment benefits and disappeared into the underground economy or hid, homeless and anonymous, in city street corners. The majority of ex-communist state's employees became part of a new "class": the "precariat."

British sociologist Guy Standing defines the "precariat" as the broad category of all those who have "no anchor of stability" and have been pushed into a "precarious existence" by the mass adoption of seductive neoliberal tenets such as "competitiveness, meritocracy, and flexibility" in capitalist economies (1, 6, 24). Although this category initially referred to "temporary or seasonal workers," it now includes all those who live with a permanent sense of vulnerability and uncertainty about their economic and social security (Standing 9–12). The modern precariat, Standing argues, needs a job to live from one day to another, is "opportunistic" (in that it accepts what is offered by the market and has no clear occupational identity), and lacks major safety nets (such as sufficient family, enterprise, and state support when in need) (11–14). The danger is that competition for survival and fear of losing one's footing take precedence over empathy for others, weakening family and community ties (Standing 20–23).

In Romania, the precariat lived in a permanent state of disavowal in the early 2000s. Those who suddenly lost the social and economic status they had built before 1989 found it difficult to adapt to the new "market" and were often pauperized, if left without family support, as is the case with the patients in *The Retirement Home* or with Mr. Tomescu in *Cigarettes and Coffee*. The young precariat either developed illusions of quick fortunes to be made from this or that temporary "opportunity," as is the case with the protagonist of *Stuff and Dough* (and many other characters in the NRC), or they became angry and let their frustrations simmer and explode.[15] One may argue that NRC is, in effect, a consistent and detailed chronicle of the rise and disillusionment of the precariat in a postnational, postpolitical world.

Stuff and Dough examines the gradual effects of the precariat's pact with the Devil for economic survival. It poses a complex dilemma about individual versus social responsibility, about the price of dreams, but, more importantly, about the very nature of good and evil in strenuous times. Ovidiu is a gullible, inexperienced, and much too self-confident young man, but he is also very easy and inexpensive prey for a network of crime that has surreptitiously reached deep into the very heart of family life. Marcel is not just any gangster in the street: he is the one who helps Ovidiu's parents when in need and seems to be a regular visitor at the house, even if Caty has misgivings about him. His initial fastidiousness about Ovidiu's six-step "mission" is rather risible and, in spite of his warning ("I am joking, but I am dead serious."), one cannot help but wonder about his own business efficacy. These are all misleading signs, but Ovidiu learns to see through them much too late. One wonders how much people like Ovidiu could "read" and understand from their economic and social environment.

The prologue establishes the parameters within which the protagonist is to evolve and indicates, to a perceptive spectator, that his indebtedness to Marcel is a *fait accompli*. The film opens with a claustrophobic shot of the apartment deli whose prospects seem to lead nowhere. (Puiu would use similar emblematic shots for all his films). A medium shot of Caty serving her clients through an opening in the grilled enclosure only further reinforces the initial sensation of imprisonment. This is the territory of the "precariat," the formerly factory-employed working class who have found themselves out of a job, and out of public consciousness, after 1989. Pushed by necessity, the more enterprising among them have redesigned their formerly private quarters, opening them to public exchanges. This invasion of the commercial realm into the familial, intimate spaces is a strategy for survival that has its risks.

Marcel Ivanov is one of them. He arrives in a silver Mercedes Cobra, an old, 1980s model, very popular in Romania in the 1990s as the car of the newly rich, but which had become so widely available by the 2000s that it had lost its prestige. The owner is, therefore, not really one of the potentates of the day, but only aspires to be one. He is wearing a gray Polo Sport coat and a golden chain around his neck, quite visible through the shirt unbuttoned down to his chest. Part of the new, capitalist order, Ivanov is not shy about it. He is immediately invited in by Caty, who also lets him go into her sleeping son's room. He wakes Ovidiu up and, throwing away a book he found on the bed, sits down, placing his hand on the boy's knee with the confident gesture of a master. He is an authoritarian father figure, one of the few in post-1989 Romanian cinema, and his origins as a longtime dealer in the communist black market are well-known to Ovidiu's father, who has a rather misguided reverence for this man. The film thus subtly comments on the rise of a profiteering class with long-established connections with the underworld, a group that has usurped both state and parental authority within the family.

Stuff and Dough is conceived as a fraught initiation journey. Puiu observes the classical plot structure—separation, transformation, return—but compresses it within twenty-four hours and narrates everything in the present tense. This strategy isolates one day in the character's life from the rest, compelling spectators to pay close attention to minute gestures and voice inflections in order to pick up clues about characters' motivations, especially because very little contextual information is provided. Such constant frustration of the viewers' desired omnipotence bars their identification with the characters, fostering their interrogation of their own perception of events.

Ovidiu is not immediately intimidated by Marcel, although he does follow his instructions to humor him. He appears naive in his self-confidence and, especially, his blindness about the true nature of the deal he has made. The few brand new toy cars strewn around the bed, his books, and posters indicate his childishness, as does his dependency on

Figure 5: The neophyte |

his mother for a pen, a clean T-shirt, or even the morning coffee. Ovidiu seems interested in recent history (the book Marcel tosses focuses on Romania's history between 1940 and 1995, and there is a second reference to 1989 in the Pink Floyd poster of *The Wall* album displayed in the room). As we soon find out, he even studied for two years at the university, but dropped out because he wanted to open his own little store. The film suggests that he has been pushed onto this path not only by economic necessity, but also by a certain bravura and desire to amount to something that he could not otherwise fulfill.

In this sense, Ovidiu represents an entire category of disenfranchised young people, oscillating, as sociologist Denise Roman suggests, between socioeconomic exclusion and integration, between rebelliousness and the need to belong (60). Roman notes that this category was particularly vulnerable after 1989: no longer the focus of state interest, they were at a disadvantage in a society dominated by "patriarchy, sexism, nationalist rhetoric, and gerontocracy" (73). Ovidiu defies everybody: he goes back to sleep when Marcel asks him to get ready; he refuses to take his mother's list; and he sends his father away when he makes plans with his mother.

Nor is he the only rebellious youngster in the film. Vali shows up at the last moment, wearing a jacket too big for his lean body and, against Ovidiu's plea, accompanied by a new girlfriend. When they are attacked by the SUV passengers, Vali curses and repeatedly provokes them. Betty herself appears meek and submissive, the "good girl" who follows the rules of the "hood," where a woman is supposed to obey and support her boyfriend (Șerban, *4 decenii* 80). However, the moment she is left alone, she disregards Ovidiu's request to guard the van and goes for an ice cream.

There is enough youthful bravado of the type one recognizes at least since *Rebel Without a Cause* (1955) or *À Bout de soufflé* (Breathless; 1960), but there is also a tacit, deeper respect for the family. Ovidiu complains about his mother, but declares that he will continue to help his parents if he gets rich. Vali helps Caty with the dishes and she relies on him when Ovidiu dismisses her requests. In spite of their rather colorful language, the three are never insolent or aggressive toward the elderly. Their rebellion is temporary, superficial, and comes with their age rather than out of any profound disagreement with the others. Standing argues that the pressure of the unstable market has led, in time, to the weakening of ties between generations, as children fear the economic commitment they may have to make (22). This is not Ovidiu's case yet. In Romania's more traditional society, the protagonist's dream is not a revolutionary one, as all he wants is a modicum of economic security: his own store, a studio, and the means to help his aging parents.

Most strikingly for the time, the film's visual regime works at once to frustrate viewers' expectations of omniscience and to focus their attention on the protagonist's vulnerability. Puiu highlights the limits of each image, as well as the act of selection performed by the camera, and, implicitly, the invisible author. The film relies on multiple frames, from the apartment's narrow hallway through which Ovidiu's interaction with Marcel, his parents, and his friends is shot, to the store opening where Caty sells her merchandise, and, of course, to the windshield and windows of the car through which the boys can have a look at the world passing them by. Like Ovidiu, viewers remain in the dark about everything that is outside the frame, that is, about everything that escapes their perception. The sensation is one of claustrophobia, of a universe isolated within its four walls, yet increasingly susceptible to the incursions of the mercantile world outside, or of the larger evil that is part of a parallel dimension. Ovidiu can anticipate nothing of what happens to him after his argument with Marcel, and he constantly reacts to events rather than take charge of them. Viewers are equally at a loss as their information is restricted to the protagonist's, whose defenselessness becomes all the more poignant.

For most of the film, Ovidiu thinks that his understanding with Marcel is temporary and merely an instrument toward his goal. He dismisses Vali, who warns him about Ivanov, only to be the target of a surprising attack on the road. This moment is particularly memorable for its haptic qualities. As they are driving along, the three pull over at the signals of a red SUV and are immediately assaulted, but manage to drive away. The scene is filmed from inside the van, where the camera has remained for the entire journey, an observer turning from one character to the other during their conversation. When they stop, the camera is initially more interested in Vali's reactions than in the SUV passengers. It becomes agitated, shaking and panning rapidly from one character to another and back to the SUV as events precipitate. This silent witness becomes, at this moment, a very palpable fourth character, conveying the stupefying nature of the events. It communicates relatively little about why the action is taking place; like the viewers and protagonists, it has no idea who attacks them or why. The camera does not even get a clear glimpse at the two assailants. What it does communicate, though, is the emotion associated with the moment: the bewilderment, shock, panic, and rage that take over the young men. The result is a visceral experience of the event that destabilizes viewers' perceptions, urges them to engage emotionally with the film, and introduces suspense. The road to Bucharest and back picks up speed for the viewers.

Ovidiu, however, still believes he is in control. He phones Marcel, irate, to threaten that they will turn around. He screams at his friends and has little patience to wait for Doncea. Most importantly, he fails to understand the wide reach of the underground "community" to which he is now bound for life. His ghastly discovery of the triple murder stuns him. Again, Puiu uses this moment to undermine narrative closure, character construction, and stylistic expectations. On his way home, Ovidiu notices the SUV stranded in the middle of a field; its passengers have been gruesomely murdered. Very rapid editing, which combines tracking shots, crossings over the 180-degree axis, rapid panning, and jump cuts, marks his discovery. The shock is palpable. With the exception of the muted dialogue among the onlookers and the few orders given by the police, there are no other sounds to highlight the event. The camera focuses on Ovidiu's tightly closed lips, his slight frowning, and distressed look. This is his direct, crude confrontation with the death of others, and the very core of the film. The next moment, he is already at the wheel and the car is turned on; from the more concerted, troubled expression on his face, one can only deduce that he has been pondering the significance of the mysterious execution. As he turns his head to the back of the van, where Vali and Betty are sleeping, carefree, Ovidiu signals his concern for his passengers. The camera returns its focus on him and, for a few more seconds, the silence, measured only by the sound of the engine, becomes even more impenetrable. Is this the moment when he understands the serious implications of his deal with Marcel? Or is he puzzled and apprehensive about what he has just seen? Does he feel responsible for his friends? Or does he want to tell them everything, but changes his mind? It is impossible to tell.

It is only at home, however, that the implications of his compromise become clearer. The narrative slowly builds toward the revelation of the widespread net of the rising mafia, of its insidiousness, cruelty, and indifference. Marcel is a nefarious figure, the very embodiment of the forces of evil within the profane world. Ovidiu's impotence when faced with situations he cannot fully fathom invites viewers' reflection on individual agency at such moments. *Stuff and Dough* is the road movie of a botched initiation, in which the antihero (the precariat) is too naive and too self-assured to understand its predicament until it is too late.

It is also the film of an unsuccessful revolt against the father. The victor is a disfigured, immoral father, the lord of an underworld. Ovidiu's parents—a strong-willed, clear-sighted, yet overburdened mother and a well-intentioned but impotent father—are so engrossed in the everyday minutiae of their small business that they cannot shield their son. Critics have noticed the "sickly symbiosis" between mother and son in the film, suggesting that Ovidiu's nickname ("Ovaru" or "Ovary") is the sign of an "incomplete gestation" (L. Dumitrescu 28). The mother, overly protective and more assertive than the father, may have failed to prepare her son for the "road," but, I would suggest, she is equally helpless when confronted with the likes of Marcel and slowly drowning under the burden of providing for the entire family. The final medium close-up profile of the young man silently eating in the kitchen at the end of the day may stir viewers' empathy for this flawed, well-intentioned human being who has bitten off much more than he could chew.

Puiu differs from previous Romanian directors in his compassionate understanding of his characters. As critics have noticed, his protagonists are no longer the radiant heroes embodying the best qualities of the nation in communism, nor the "debased," "subhuman" figures that populated the 1990s "gutter" or "screaming" cinema (Pop 57). Nor are they influenced by the qualities associated with the typical Hollywood hero, whose ruggedness, bravery, and defiance give him the upper hand in most situations. For the first time, the people on screen look, behave, and talk exactly like the people in front of the screen, sometimes too much so (Sava, *O istorie,* vol. 1: 285).

A few critics particularly commended *Stuff and Dough* for the accuracy with which the actors were able to construct their characters

(Şerban, *4 decenii* 222). This accomplishment is all the more important considering that the actors were recent film school graduates with little or no experience on the set. Not only do they speak the language of the streets with remarkable nonchalance, but they also seem to inhabit their characters with no reserve. For all three young actors, this was their first feature, and they have declared that Puiu's working style profoundly influenced their careers (Chirilov and Sandu 51–52). "We had the good chance of being formed by Cristi Puiu. . . . You cannot lie in his films. Why do I say that [Vali] is one of my best roles—and it is a bit unpleasant for me to say it? Because it is the only film in which I cannot catch myself exposed. It is the only one," declares Dragoș Bucur ("RetrospecTIFF").[16] The actors have described a very rigorous rehearsal practice, with minute attention given to the rhythm of gestures and lines in front of the camera (Chirilov and Sandu 52). The naturalism of the acting further reinforced the "roughness" of the film, conferring upon it a documentary aura and the impression that one is watching life unfolding.

Puiu's debut feature was ignored at the annual ceremony of the Romanian Filmmakers' Union (Sava, *O istorie,* vol. 1: 156–57). Having been screened in Cannes, *Stuff and Dough* traveled to a few other international festivals (Cottbus, Buenos Aires, Thessaloniki), where it was acknowledged for its social insight and efficient use of cinematic techniques ("FIPRESCI Awards"). In spite of the difficulty with which the film was made, Puiu had refused major compromises to his vision about the relationship between cinema, reality, and spectators. His close observation of the life in one of the many neighborhoods of a postcommunist metropolis captures the surreptitious spread of the underground world and its slow engulfing of the precariat classes. The handheld, mobile camera engaged viewers' perceptions and critical faculties, urging them to reflect on the fate of everyday individuals when confronted with historical forces beyond their control.

Fathers and Sons: *Cigarettes and Coffee*

Puiu's first major international recognition came with the Golden Bear award he received in 2004 for *Cigarettes and Coffee;* it was Romania's first such prize in forty years.[17] The organizers introduced the short as representing one of the "countries which have rarely participated in the [Berlin film] festival" (the other was Macedonia) ("Jan 22 2004"). To foreign eyes, this achievement may have indicated the existence of a coherent system of support for young filmmakers that had finally yielded "results." The reality was quite different. Puiu and the upcoming NRC directors made films against the opposition and even economic sabotage of the establishment.

The early 2000s witnessed the first generational clashes in Romanian cinematography. The NCC, the only institution responsible for the selection of projects to be financed, was marred by corruption and nepotism (Sava, *O istorie,* vol. 1: 77, 211). By 2003, the future NRC directors had written public letters of protest and had participated in several televised debates regarding the new law for cinematography under discussion in the Parliament (Sava, *O istorie,* vol. 1: 215–16). In the most infamous of them, Sergiu Nicolaescu, the most prodigious director of the communist era and a parliamentarian for the Social Democrat Party in power, confronted Puiu and Mungiu with the condescension of a father bothered by two children's insubordination (Tuca). At the root of the conflict was the question of value. To the "fathers," cinema was a *national* enterprise supposed to make a profit, educate the masses, and promote a positive image of the country abroad. To the "sons," it was an *individual* form of expression and investigation, capable of fostering cross-cultural dialogue. Although the ex-communist "notables" would still hold the reins of the industry for a few more years, their time was coming to an end.

The question of father and sons is at the very heart of *Cigarettes and Coffee,* an apparently modest film, which, nevertheless, bears considerable symbolic weight. Puiu subtly indicates two of his spiritual fathers for this project, anchoring it in both local and global tradition. *Cigarettes and Coffee* is dedicated to Bela (Willie) Molnar, Jim Jarmusch's antihero in *Stranger than Paradise* (1984), a film Puiu credits (together with Cassavetes's *A Woman under the Influence* [1974]) with his change of direction from painting to cinema. The 2004 short film is a wink at Jarmusch's *Coffee and Cigarettes* (2003), composed of a series of vignettes shot over a seventeen-year period, in which different personalities engage in sometimes contradictory, sometimes nonsensical conversation. What traverses the screen is a glimpse of the characters' nature and interaction: the strangers who talk past each other; the Brits who drink tea; or the "cousins" who love to irritate each other. The coffee and cigarettes in Puiu's film are not to be consumed, but to be given as bribe to others, and the dialogue does not reveal the humor and the absurdity of everyday life—the "nothingness" made famous by *Seinfeld* (1989–1998)—but the deep gap between two generations and two modes of being.

The film's other precursor is Stere Gulea's *The Moromete Family*, an adaptation of a famous Romanian novel that explored the rift torn between a small landowner and his sons by the advent of communism. The sons rob and abandon their father in order to move to the city. Finished in 1985, *The Moromete Family* was repeatedly denied a release by the communist censors for its anti-Party innuendoes and daring neorealist black-and-white aesthetics. Puiu intended *Cigarettes and Coffee* as a tribute, and he initially cast Victor Rebengiuc and Ionel Mihăilescu, two of the actors in Gulea's movie, as the father and son in his own short. Tomescu Sr. (Victor Rebengiuc) might very well be the revolting son in the earlier film; the march of history has caught him unaware, just as it did his "father" in the 1950s. It will do the same to young and impetuous Vlad Tomescu (Mimi Brănescu).

Cigarettes and Coffee neither condemns nor endorses the effects of this march. The premise of the father-son conversation was quite familiar to Romanians at the time: the father has asked the son for help finding a new job. His company—the fictive "UCECHIM" that sounds quite similar to ICECHIM, the national institute for research, once under the patronage of Elena Ceaușescu herself—has been laying people off, so he is fired only two years before his retirement age. A state company, UCECHIM has seen better days, when its employees were provided with a hot meal (Mr. Tomescu used to transport, load, and unload the food) and now it is to be sold to foreign investors. This privatization seems to follow a controlled bankruptcy, as one could only wonder why foreign investors would want to buy an enterprise no longer capable of maintaining its employees.

The film alludes to a scandalous reality of the time. Many quick privatizations were questionable, especially when, after teetering on the brink of bankruptcy, businesses were "saved" at the last moment and either turned profitable soon thereafter or sold as real estate. Such deals were often made under the protection of political figures, who accumulated so much economic power that they "earned" the title of "barons," a term that harks back to the Middle Ages. The "feudalization" of the country was the product of a system that worked on "connections," was partly a legacy of the past—many of the new "barons" had been in privileged positions before 1989—and was both an effect of, and a further cause for, the weakening of the state's authority (Verdery 205–08). The ex-communist patriarchal state was being cannibalized by its many minions.

The new capitalist economy profited from the demise of its predecessor by abandoning those incapable of defending themselves. Like the patients in *The Retirement Home* and Ovidiu's parents in *Stuff and Dough,* Mr. Tomescu has suddenly been left to fend for himself, with no support, and no particular qualification, after thirty-one years in the service of the same company. The restaurant where he meets his son Vlad is named "Graceland," a rather ironic metonymical reference to the state that has neither compassion nor grace toward its precariat classes. Graceland is also the mythical place of consumerist pleasures in whose decomposing shadow relationships enter their own agonizing phase (as it also was in Jarmusch's *Mystery Train* [1989], to which Puiu probably alludes).

Cigarettes and Coffee is an exercise in austere, effective aesthetic expression. Classical editing, theatricality, and repetition are instrumental in this regard. The film opens with a long shot from inside the restaurant toward the street, where the older man initially passes right by the glass door only to return and, a bit puzzled, step in. When he finally recognizes his son and walks toward him, the camera pans left to reveal Vlad, probably in his early thirties, seated in a chair by the window and reading some documents. A suit that looks rather big on him and a briefcase that is not quite the leather one associated with the executive classes indicate that he enjoys a better situation than others, but aspires to more. Compared to the father, whose old cap, gray grocery bag (a relic from communist times), and outdated clothes betray his meager, yet decent means, the son is the epitome of the "entrepreneur": superficially polished (he eats his pie with a fork and knife), always in a rush, and quite self-assured. This is the new, upwardly mobile class, ready to compete and deft at using all possible connections to get where they want to go, yet still economically and socially vulnerable and, therefore, still part of the precariat. If Ovidiu in *Stuff and Dough* is an innocent trapped against his better judgment, Vlad is quite aware of how things work: by bribery.

In the next medium long shot, father and son are symmetrically positioned at each end of the restaurant table, with two curtains adorning the edges of the frame. This theatrical image is repeated at crucial moments, marking the different emotional layers of their interaction: their awkwardness when they meet; the son's growing impatience with the father; the old man's reluctant consent to the job he is "offered"; and their rushed farewell. The film, thus, finely traces the gradual deterioration of family relationships into expedient exchanges through which money and services have replaced affection. The fixed camera, detectable only at the beginning and end of the film, is the silent witness of this metamorphosis.

Vlad is eager to consume as much as possible—information, food, drinks—in as little time as possible, not only because this meeting may very well annoy him, but also because he is in a rush to get more. The clean, almost invisible montage, in the absence of a non-diegetic, interfering soundtrack, concentrates attention on the characters themselves. Pop notes that Vlad is the "metonymic representation of the capitalist consumerism," and I would add that this is a particular type of consumerism generated by penury and frustration (137). Vlad's is a consumerism of recovery: he desires more not only because he is young, but also because he, like most other citizens, was deprived of much of it as a child. Furthermore, his dessert of choice is not some exotic cake, but apple pie, a staple in most houses during communism, and, possibly, Vlad's "madeleine" of the childhood he wants overwritten.

Especially unpleasant is his patronizing approach to the old man. Much of the dialogue relies on repetition and reinforcement; the discussion about the father's possible new job is quite suggestive in this sense. Vlad starts by asking him if he still wants to be a van driver, but makes sure to point out that he is in no position to choose, "A van driver or will you settle for something else?" When Mr. Tomescu, big-eyed and a bit baffled, replies, in half a voice, "A driver," his son addresses him as if he were a child, "And if I can't get you a driver's job? That is what I am asking. If I can't get you a driver's job, will you take anything else?" The father continues to be completely blind to his son's implied request that he reconsider and, innocently, replies, "A van driver. But I'll be ok working as a pick-up driver." The bitter humor in this wry dialogue springs from the father's utter bewilderment at the rapid social transformations around him. Just as he had barely missed the restaurant because the building "used to be something else," he now fully misunderstands his son because he refuses to believe that his longtime qualifications do not amount to much, or that his yuppie Vlad cannot help him as he wishes. The son explodes, "Dad, a job as a van driver I cannot find. I cannot find a job as a van driver. I am asking you: can you do something else?" The young man's frustration is itself a form of emotional blindness: he is incapable of understanding that the night guard job he has found is, in fact, a demotion and, therefore, quite a blow to the old man's ego. When he, later, questions his dad's desire to work, the latter replies, "Vlad, dear, I just cannot not work." The dignity of being employed and providing for his wife, even if not completely, is essential to this man's identity, and much at odds with the son's neoliberal philosophy of market "flexibility." Puiu depicts the old generation's situation with empathy for the sense of self-worth and security it stands to lose.

Neither is the portrait of the young son less nuanced. Vlad is gruff and occasionally irritated, but not completely insensitive. He pays for his parents' bills and his mother's medicine. He asks his dad, possibly out of politeness, if he wants anything to eat and is refused twice. His mistake is to be content with the father's refusal rather than understand that it may be a matter of pride and embarrassment. Vlad also points out that his dad's new job may mean that his paralyzed mother will need a caretaker, which a night guard salary (or that of a van driver for that matter) could not afford. The son seems rational and straightforward, qualities that do not necessarily make him callous, but only more pragmatic and better adapted to the times.

The father is the opposite. He lives psychologically isolated within a patriarchal, slowly dying world, whose economy is one of subsistence, but whose benefits lie in its subjects' sense of security. In the new world, he seems lost. He barely sits down when the waiter presents him with a long list of beer and water brands, which renders him speechless. The same confusion is visible when he buys instant coffee—very popular in communism—rather than Lavazza, the imported coffee his son required.

Figure 6: The precariat |

Or, maybe, he only bought what he could afford. There is not much difference between his past (when he may have had the money but could not find the products) and his present (when he does not have the money and cannot buy the products) in this respect.

But knowledge of brand-name coffees was never Mr. Tomescu's purpose in life. He has been taking care of his paralyzed wife with unstinting devotion, as viewers can infer from the contents of his bag: celery for a soup and a wooden massage device to give some comfort to his spouse. Vlad seems puzzled by the "machine," so the old man shows him how to use it. This is the only moment when the two seem emotionally intimate, but it is very brief. If the son dismisses this wooden mechanism as inconsequential to his life, the father perceives it as an instrument of affection. This is a very brief glimpse at people's capacity for connection, and deeper ties, to each other buried deep under layers of social pressures and responsibilities.

Mr. Tomescu's realization that nothing has changed since 1989 is almost a relief: "In the end, nothing has changed: it's like in the old times, with coffee and cigarettes." Knowledge of the "system" at least gives him some sense of control. "Well, can't you see nothing has changed? It's like in the old times: with coffee and cigarettes," the son echoes condescendingly. Another instance in which the short film relies on repetition as a means of emphasizing difference, this dialogue signals a major transfor-

Figure 7: The "machine" |

mation in Romanian society. The practice of bribery remained the same, yet the significance of the bribe was different. In communism, coffee and cigarettes were rare, luxury products, difficult to procure; when offered, they had value in themselves, in that they could be consumed by the lucky recipients, or they had value as objects of exchange, when they were "re-gifted" further on. After 1989, when coffee and cigarettes were available everywhere, their connotation changed. Paradoxically, they remained important in winning the graces of the powerful in that their absence was perceived as a gesture of disrespect. This is why the son insists on a particular type of coffee and cigarettes—more expensive and, therefore, more valuable as a gesture—and this is what the father cannot understand. These two men, whose worldviews are at odds, are both victims of the new economy, yet remain unable to relate to each other.

Critics have noticed that, in Puiu's films, as in many of the NRC films, father figures are never balanced: they are either degraded, weak, absent, or, simply, authoritarian and destructive (Pop 125–26). The father in *Cigarettes and Coffee* may be financially dependent on the son, but there is dignity in his refusal of Vlad's offer of pie or a car ride. He is among the luckier few of the precariat because he can still count on his children's help, but the story may be much different for Vlad's generation.

Puiu has been described as an "angry young director," a hint at the similarity between his attitude and that of the British filmmakers of the 1950s, who also rebelled against their fathers' artistic choices (Pop 119). There is more in the Romanian's relationship with the past, be it of the country itself, of cinema as an art, and even his own personal past, than a simple rejection of "fathers." There is appreciation and care for some of their legacy, in spite of the youthful impetus to be rid of it.

Having won in Berlin, *Cigarettes and Coffee* was received, in Romania, as a "great triumph" by the young critics, who appreciated it for its complex insight into the father-son relationship (Blaga, "Mare triumf"; Gorzo, "Top 5"). Puiu's astute choice of subject matter and style reflected on Romanian realities at the time, but it also echoed a much wider, global concern for the expanding generational divide and the fate of both parents and children.[18] A few months later, Cătălin Mitulescu's *Trafic* (Traffic; 2004), another short exploring the relationship between a young father and his little daughter, won the Palme d'Or in the short film section, as well. These were the first two films to attract international attention to the Romanian directors and, indirectly, to open many doors for other projects.

Regarding the Death of Others: *The Death of Mr. Lazarescu*

2005 would mark another landmark moment for Romanian cinema, and Cristi Puiu was, again, its architect. His second feature, *Mr. Lazarescu*, was hailed in Cannes for the quality of its acting, the attention paid to re-creating the protagonist's social reality, and its dark humor (Vodă). This film made such an impression on the local and international critics that Puiu was deemed the founder of a new era by critic Alex. Leo Șerban (who separated the entire history of Romanian cinema into "BC and AC: before and after Cristi [Puiu]") ("Bridging the Gap" 12). Others have also noted the dramatic influence of Puiu's aesthetics on the new generation, some with humor (as did director Corneliu Porumboiu in *12:08 East of Bucharest* [*A fost sau n-a fost?* 2006]), some with critical acuity (Romanian critics Șerban and Andrei Gorzo have underscored the radical influence of *Mr. Lazarescu* on Cristian Mungiu's and Radu Muntean's second features, *4 Months, 3 Weeks, and 2 Days* [*4 luni, 3 săptămâni și 2 zile*; 2007] and *The Paper Will Be Blue* [*Hârtia va fi albastră*; 2006] respectively) (Şerban, *4 decenii* 57; Gorzo, *Lucruri* 257). One should note, however, that, although stylistically most NRC films can be traced back to Puiu's 2005 feature, they embody very different approaches to cinema. What remains indisputable, however, is that *Mr. Lazarescu* was the start of a "revolution."

To make the film, Puiu had to struggle again against the inertia of the industry. The script was initially rejected in the NCC competition (Sava, *O istorie,* vol. 2: 121). He appealed to the Minister of Culture, Răzvan Theodorescu, who, recognizing the importance of the 2004 Golden Bear award, secured the funding from the Center (Sava, *O istorie,* vol. 2: 121). Without the recognition of the international festival industry, what was to become the cult film of the NRC might not have been made.

The incompetence and power abuse surrounding *Mr. Lazarescu* reflected, in a way, the old generation's frustration in the early 2000s. By 2004, the gradual reduction in the state's support for the cinema industry and the controversial policies regarding the privatization of the ex-communist studios and theater network had had disastrous effects on production. Of 254 theaters in 2001, only eighty-four survived by 2005 and seventy-two by 2007 (Radu 138). More than 60 percent of the releases were Hollywood-based (Radu 86). Under such circumstances, the NCC became the major, if not only, source of funding and cultural endorsement. The Center allocated a zero-interest credit, which was to be paid in ten years or else the film would become state property (Pricop 114–17). At least twenty legislative changes were made between 2002 and 2006, many of which were just cosmetic fixes undertaken under pressure from NRC directors, and had little influence on the NCC's actual practices ("Istoric").

This constant struggle against a slow and stubborn institution prompted many young filmmakers to set up their own companies. The success of the NRC is, in part, the success of directors such as Cristian Mungiu, Tudor Giurgiu, or Cătălin Mitulescu (to name only a few) as entrepreneurs. In 2004 Puiu, his wife Anca, and Alexandru Munteanu established Mandragora. The company was to endorse a new type of appreciation for cinema in a country in which, for many years, films had been perceived, and used, as instruments of propaganda and facile entertainment (Gilbey 30). *Mr. Lazarescu* was its first production.

The 2005 film is also the first in the *Six Tales from the Outskirts of Bucharest* series. The collection was intended to explore the value, limits, and representation of love: love for humanity (in *Mr. Lazarescu*); love in a couple (the focus of *Aurora*); erotic love; love for one's offspring; love for one's friends; and love of success (Holden E5). *Mr. Lazarescu* is loosely based on the real case of Constantin Nica, a fifty-two-year-old homeless man found dead on a street in Bucharest on April 23, 1997, wearing pajama bottoms and an IV. He had been "shipped" between four hospitals and refused admission because he was drunk and was not accompanied by any relatives (Bălan).[19] The only one to be convicted of his death was the paramedic, which Puiu found outrageous (Gilbey 30).

The media discussion of the case fired the director's memories of his own brushes with death in the 1990s, after an acute appendicitis or when he was diagnosed with Mallory-Weiss syndrome (a disease that involves vomiting blood), a diagnosis that Lazarescu's neighbor freely "offers" as an explanation for the older man's pain. Puiu's 1998 experience in the Craiova retirement home also inspired him. The act of dying, the spatial closeness and yet psychological distance from the moribund of all those whose lives are not in danger, and the unyielding passing of time are recurrent *topoi* in his work.

For the script, Puiu collaborated with Rădulescu, with whom he also worked on *Niki and Flo* (Niki Ardelean, colonel în rezervă; 2003, dir. Lucian Pintilie), and *Offset* (2006, dir. Didi Danquart). All films are character studies of strong-minded individuals who are, somehow, put at a disadvantage by their own past choices and by present circumstances over which they have little, if any, control. Shot in thirty-nine nights in various hospitals in Bucharest, *Mr. Lazarescu* is no exception. The title gives away the plot even before audiences get into the theater. One knows what will happen and to whom. Puiu, however, turns the experience into a 150-minute-long ordeal of a man shipped, for six hours, among different hospitals as his consciousness deteriorates beyond recovery. Lazarescu (Ioan Fiscuteanu) is a sixty-three-year-old retiree, who calls the ambulance one evening because he feels weak. His neighbors keep him company, but do not hear him cry for help when he falls in the bathroom. Mioara Avram (Luminița Gheorghiu), the paramedic who arrives to help him, is a woman about his age; she takes his pulse and gives him blood-thinning medicine before she decides to take him to the hospital. The first doctor who consults him delivers the right diagnosis (hepatic cirrhosis) and, after scolding him for drinking, expedites him to a different hospital for an in-depth examination. Over twenty victims of a bus accident on the outskirts of Bucharest soon overwhelm the system, and Lazarescu is sent from hospital to hospital for more tests until, in the morning, the last doctor agrees to perform the surgery to address the stroke that has rendered him unconscious in the meantime. Viewers' expectations of a clear progression of events and climax are constantly eschewed as information accumulates slowly, doctors repeat the same ritual in each hospital, and suspense is prolonged with each visit only to be frustrated yet again. As critics have suggested, even those who may have hoped, in spite of the title, that things would end up well for the protagonist, root for his demise by the end, if only to escape the wheels of bureaucracy (Gilbey 28). Lazarescu's death will, however, remain beyond the time frame of the film itself, as a final denial of spectatorial expectations.

It is, paradoxically, the life on screen that eventually engages viewers' interest. A retired engineer, the protagonist is a member of the "intellectual" classes—as his neighbor Sandu (Doru Ana) defines him—of whom much was expected during communism. In a country where building factories was number one on the dictator's list, engineers enjoyed social and economic prominence and prestige. 1989 radically changed their condition. Many had to requalify, be content with a meager income, or were simply fired shortly before their retirement (a situation that put them in the same boat with the ex-working classes, as was the case of Tomescu Sr.). By 2006, the number of pensioners (six million) overtook that of employees (four million) (Boia, *România* 196). Retirees suffered from poverty more than other social categories (De Vos and Sandefur 23). About half of them lived with a relative and very few (less than 1 percent) lived in an institution (De Vos and Sandefur 27, 30). Puiu's sensitivity to the fate of these abandoned "parents" and their legacy would inform all his work.

Lazarescu is one of them. His wife died eight years before and his only daughter lives in Toronto.[20] His sister Eva and brother-in-law Virgil live far away from Bucharest and, over the phone, reproach him for wasting his money, and theirs, on booze. Three cats keep him company in an apartment frozen in the 1980s and the days of Kim Wilde's glory (as posters of the singer indicate). Lazarescu eats meats and cheese, and drinks Mastropol, a home-made vanilla-based brandy. One senses that he has seen better days and that alcohol is only a means to pass, and measure, time. Bothered by a persistent headache, he calls the emergency service and pours half a glass. He drinks slowly and waits for the effect. He gets ready to take another sip when time hurries; a cut to a few moments later reveals him slumped over the bandages for his varicose veins. The only help comes from his neighbors, Sandu and Miki (Dana Dogaru), who bring him food and medication (a kind gesture that, in the long run, only worsens his condition). They also scold him for drinking (while making plans to buy wine themselves) and express their disgust at his cohabitation with the cats. By the time the ambulance arrives, viewers have become privy to the small universe within the building, where everybody thinks they know everything about everybody else.

The camera filters all this information for the viewer. It is there, with the antihero as he calls the ambulance, and follows him relentlessly, rarely wandering off. So obsessive is its gaze that it eschews all other "rules" regarding framing: it "chops off" heads and bodies, it pans left and right, following the characters as they speak, and it lingers around Lazarescu when he is asked to sign a disclaimer. Puiu would later consider the camera's mobility a liability to his intentions because it gave the impression of omniscience and was not sufficiently conducive to an awareness of one's limited perception of the world. This invisible,

Figure 8: Calling for help |

palpable witness is, nevertheless, irritating in its inability to "see" it all, disconcerting in its constant movement, and capricious in its choices. For viewers accustomed to omniscient narratives, it is frustrating that essential information is occluded from view, as is the case with Lazarescu's fall in the bathroom; did he, indeed, fall and get a hematoma, or did his already-existing hematoma cause him to lose his balance? It is impossible to know because the camera "stays" in the living room, more interested in the conversation among the neighbors (like everybody else around Lazarescu, even this extra witness has "better" things to do). This fictional, non-diegetic observer is endowed with its own subjectivity and viscerally connected to the spectators' perception.

Character complexity is one of Puiu's narrative pursuits. For the first fifty minutes of the film, very little happens: a man feels sick; he calls for an ambulance; and he is taken to the hospital. Puiu constructs Lazarescu's world with great attention to the smallest details, carefully contextualized with an anthropologist's eye for "thick description" (Geertz 10). The phrase, launched by Clifford Geertz, refers to the in-depth, multilayered observation and interpretation of a culture. Geertz notes, "Doing ethnography is like trying to read (in the sense of 'construct a reading of') a manuscript—foreign, faded, full of ellipses, incoherencies, suspicious emendations, and tendentious commentaries, but written not in conventionalized graphs of sound but in transient examples of shaped behavior" (10). One may argue the same about Puiu's "study" of Lazarescu. The film adopts an ethnographic approach in which the "subject" is closely followed in his own "environment" without his awareness of the "researcher" (the director and the viewer) behind the lens. The impression of real life invading the screen is all the more powerful as the film "feels" as if it were a documentary, in which the camera functions as a silent, invisible witness, with shaking hands and a desire to see everything. Puiu's intention is, thus, double: to create a rich fictional world that is faithful, in its intimate details, to his own perception of this milieu, and to introduce a documentary-style observer (the camera) in order to emphasize the subjective, limited, fictional nature of any attempted perception, depiction, or re-creation of life.[21]

The result of his attention to detail, Puiu hopes, will be a more direct relationship between the film and the viewer fostered by the latter's recognition of the world shared with the protagonist. Writing about war photos, Susan Sontag noted the necessity that they be devoid of the appearance of artificiality in order to be believable: ". . . [P]eople want the weight of witnessing without the taint of artistry, which is equated with insincerity or mere contrivance" (26). Artistry implies a focus on aesthetics, and on their effect on the viewers, rather than on the suffering human being in front of the lens. Puiu seeks the same sobriety of style that Sontag demands of war photos because, for him, too, the attention needs to be on the pain of others. The impression of rough, unprocessed experience in *Mr. Lazarescu* confers legitimacy upon its depiction of suffering and conveys gravity to the solitary act of dying.

That *Mr. Lazarescu* is a work of fictional ethnography becomes evident in the constant suggestions that little in the world on screen is to be taken at face value. Especially poignant is the emphasis on the characters' largely unknowable private histories. Puiu subtly hints at the protagonist's fall from grace. Viewers' first impression is of a disheveled, grumpy loner, but the man is more than the building's drunk. He tenderly cares for his pets and the many plants taking over his daughter's room. He is wounded by his child's absence and his sister's reproaches, but he tries to protect both when he initially refuses to reveal the seriousness of his situation. A combination of pride, hurt, and love has turned him into a solitary, self-reliant curmudgeon, but one has reason to wonder if that has always been his character. He becomes cantankerous only when he thinks he has been mistreated, especially when he perceives it as an attack on his honor. He is particularly belligerent when he is accused of abuse against his wife and daughter by a doctor who has just met him.

Critics have described Lazarescu as an antihero, "incapable of action, of changing his destiny," a weak father, of whom there are many in the NRC (Pop 98).[22] He may be doomed because of his affliction, but he would fight it if he could. He stands up to go home in the first medical ward, when a doctor insults him. He hints to the paramedic that his sister will reward her, monetarily, for her help, fully aware that he is on his own in a system in which bribery has been institutionalized as a form of copayment.[23] And he is right: Dr. Mirică's (Mimi Brănescu) first question is whether Lazarescu is accompanied by anyone (read: anyone who could pay a bribe).[24] "I don't want" are the patient's last words, as he pushes away the consent forms. What he does not want is the risk that he would become paralyzed, a risk he understood fairly well but, given his state, cannot discuss further. James Quandt has argued that Lazarescu's journey is one of "escalating loss—of control, identity, speech, hope" (81). The most profound injury is his loss of dignity, I would suggest. He is steadily deprived of the little respectability he has won in life: his status, his family's confidence, the doctors' consideration (even those who treat him well address him as if he were a child), and, eventually, his capacity to fight back. Like Mr. Popescu in *The Retirement Home,* Lazarescu will end up spoon-fed and washed by nurses. He becomes incontinent and progressively loses his consciousness, but his is not a desired withdrawal from the world; it is one that he can no longer control. Lazarescu is a weak father because he is dying.

Neither is Mioara, his confidant, a one-dimensional character. The paramedic who accompanies the protagonist on his distressing journey is overeager to help, but she gets involved too much and with negative effects on her patient. As the doctors repeatedly point out, she does not possess the knowledge necessary to diagnose Lazarescu properly, but she makes decisions and imparts them with absolute confidence of her authority in the matter. The glucose and vitamins she injects only worsen his situation, and she dismisses Lazarescu's complaints about his headache as "psychosomatic." In spite of the sometimes abrupt, even aggressive manner in which doctors comment on each other's actions and opinions, their observations are correct (and Puiu's "thick description" is rich in this respect, too). When she reaches the third hospital, at 3:00 A.M., Mioara is exhausted and she infuriates Dr. Mirică, who takes his time consulting the half-comatose patient only because he wants to badger her. If the film is a crash-course on mortality, by the end, Mioara is most conscious of its proximity. She has gulped pill after pill for her liver pain, has bumped into the bloodied, young victims of the bus accident, and has been taunted and harassed by most of the doctors. This woman is, in effect, Lazarescu's alter ego and she becomes increasingly aware of it (Brooke 69). As he is finally being prepared for surgery, she lingers. "Watch his legs; he has varicose [veins]," she tells the two nurses, in a motherly impulse. Like her ward, Mioara is a complex figure, "drawn" with the precision of an experienced painter (and Puiu's accuracy has been compared to that of Bruegel) (Gilbey 30; Quandt 81).

Such "thick description" of the medical world was the subject of debates in Romania. The pre-1989 bribe economy—the effect of a scarcity of medicine and technology—found fertile ground in postcommunism, when an indifferent, often absent state oversaw the gradual deterioration of the health care structure. In the early 2000s, most hospitals were state-owned and doctors' salaries reached indecent depths.[25] Bribes "supplemented" a physician's income, but became especially pernicious when patients were neglected in the absence of such "payments." Critics interpreted Puiu's film as a condemnation of the system, which they perceived as detrimental to the country's "image" abroad (Gilbey 30). No doctor, however, asks for a bribe and only one inquires about Lazarescu's family in the film; others even do small favors for the paramedic. Furthermore, foreign critics have noticed the affinities between Lazarescu's situation and the state of similar services in their own countries, especially when overwhelmed by a traumatic incident (Brooke 68–69; Sklar 63). The film, therefore, does not focus on exposing the flaws of a system but represents it only as one of the many other factors on Lazarescu's journey.

Many have related Puiu's work to Frederick Wiseman's *Hospital* (1970) or to documentaries by Raymond Depardon (Gilbey 28; Holden E5; Quandt 81; Hoberman 232). Indeed, Wiseman and Depardon were the focus of Puiu's and his cinematographer's (Oleg Mutu) analysis in preparation for *Mr. Lazarescu*. The Romanian differs from them in one fundamental way, however: his film primarily records the interaction among different people rather than the relationships established between an institution and its subjects.

Furthermore, Puiu relies on hapticity to "move" viewers. It is not necessary for Lazarescu's neighbors to comment on the stale odor of his apartment: one can sense it in the food left out in the open in his kitchen; the yellowish linens on his couch and the bed where two cats sleep; the walls plastered with old posters; or the stuffed toys crowded in his daughter's former bedroom. The rather impressionistic use of color only deepens the impact of the events. The reddish tint in the apartment gives way to the greenish hues inside the ambulance, where the patient keeps spewing out his bile, and, eventually, to the whites and blues of the hospitals, where disease, death, and chlorine meet each other in the soft moans of patients, occasional screams of pain, and the doctors' detachment. As the protagonist's body begins to spill out, and neither bandages nor will can keep liquids in, images themselves bleed, impregnating viewers' sight. The physical sensations associated with these moving frames further reinforce the impression of genuine experience. The film's faithful simulation of the emotion attached to one's perception of a dying man thus contributes to its empathetic gaze.

Mr. Lazarescu does make some pertinent comments on the organization of the few hospitals it "visits," on the coteries that inhabit them, and on their inheritance of practices and mores. Lazarescu, Dante Remus, is a "client" or "the accused," as doctors and nurses refer to him; in their world, his kin are in great supply, but doctors are few and mighty. Each hospital, symbolically a terrace of Purgatory, is a world unto itself, with its own hierarchies, but with little respect for patients or the state (as the owner). There is no communication with other institutions, always perceived as lacking and incompetent. Within their own microcosms, doctors, residents, nurses, and attendants rank higher than the paramedics and the ambulance drivers. "We are all medical staff here," Mioara reproachfully tells Dr. Mirică and the resident; "No, we are medical staff of different qualification, nurse," he puts her in her place. Not that Mioara bonds with other nurses, who also reject her (with the exception of a friend she meets in one cabinet). Hospitals appear as small worlds onto themselves, as Lazarescu and his guide are fated to face their self-isolation and indifference.

Again, Puiu's reliance on thick description renders the situation more complicated than at first view. Everybody seems to help Mioara at the University Hospital, even if they do not know her. A couple (played by Puiu's own parents) agree to let Lazarescu be consulted before them, out of compassion. Three doctors pull a few strings to get him a CAT scan and the necessary surgery, which fails because of the many casualties that have just arrived. Even in one of the most modern hospitals and with the most helpful staff, the odds are against this patient. It is not the wheels of any institution but the wheels of time that betray him. Thick description becomes, therefore, the instrument through which characters and situations become too difficult to assess, as they keep multiplying and do not fit into clear-cut categories. One is always aware of the more left out of frame.

This impression of authenticity is also achieved through the further fragmentation of the information viewers receive by means of very visible gaps in the narrative, a strategy that would become even more troubling in *Aurora*. It is unclear how much time elapses between Lazarescu's first call to the ambulance and, for example, the moment he ties his bandages over his varicose veins. The cut in the otherwise real-time observation of the character makes visible this passage, as it does every time there is a transition between the interior of the ambulance and the reception wards of the four hospitals. The same effect is accomplished through the constant emphasis on truncated life stories. Conversations and relationships always raise more questions than they answer. For example, Leo (Gabriel Spahiu), Mișu (Dragoș Bucur), another ambulance driver, and Mioara discuss the case of a corrupt doctor, but viewers are left wanting more. The relationship between the two doctors—Gina Filip (Clara Vodă) and Dragoș Popescu (Adrian Titieni)—who help Lazarescu is very ambiguous: are they friends who just like teasing each other? Lovers? Spouses?[26] There is a "thickness" of detail that overwhelms and refuses closure.

Thick description is supplemented by allegory, which connects the spatially and temporally confined world of the film to an even larger reality beyond it. The suggested presence of forces beyond one's control emphasizes human vulnerability. Repetition and symbolism complicate the narrative. Four times the patient is "shipped," at night, through dark streets, by a rather snappy, know-it-all Charon, aka Leo, the ambulance driver. And four times the doctors follow the same ritual: interview, consultation, and blood, speech, and vision tests. Commenting on being "inspired" by the American series *ER* (1994–2009), Puiu noted, "In my country, doctors and everyone else live in slow motion, as if they were on Valium and still had 500 years to live" (Hoberman 232). Time seems to be standing still, and not only because the film avoids rapid cutting and an overdramatic soundtrack. From the first minute the patient steps into a hospital, he stays in line. There are lines everywhere: in front of the hospital, where paramedics have to wait for approval, in front of the doctors' cabinets, inside the doctors' cabinets. . . . Individuals seem dwarfed, swallowed by a system with the strength of a Leviathan, with which they are, nevertheless, very familiar.

The protagonist's pretentious name is a mishmash of references. "Remus," the name of the twin who died and was forgotten as his brother Romulus founded Rome, is a stand-in for the anonymous many whose lives are not recorded in history. Lazarescu (Lazarus) suggests a possible resurrection in a world beyond the physical one. Dante is a double figure: both mortal as a human being and immortal as an artist. Puiu's protagonist is caught on a limb between two worlds, unable to leave one and not yet welcomed in the other one. His wandering through the maze of emergency rooms is "guided" by a rather ambiguous, inexperienced "Virgil" in the person of Mioara.[27] Her name reminds Romanian viewers of a very popular ballad, "The Little Ewe" ("Miorița"), in which a shepherd is warned of his imminent death by an enchanted sheep, with whom he also leaves instructions about his funeral. The crossing over is depicted as a wedding, with Death as a princess-bride. Puiu hints at Lazarescu's role as a "groom" in the last sequence, when the old man is shaved for surgery (shaving is part of the nuptial rituals in Romania) and one of the nurses addresses him as "bridegroom." Mioara and her patient are never aware of such connotations. The close presence of the sacred, as well as the constant allusions to mythical figures and initiation rites confer a universal significance upon the fate of Lazarescu, whose human frailty and journey into the beyond are what each viewer is to expect; such is the ultimate epiphany of the film.

One of the means by which such epiphany is negotiated is the illusion of real-time duration. The insertion of time into the very weave of the image concentrates attention on the characters' smallest gestures, facial expressions, and possible emotions and thoughts. Of poignant effect is the very last image of the film, when a shaved Lazarescu slowly turns his gaze to the camera and then back up, keeping this last experience to himself. Viewers can only wonder if, having watched this man for such a long time, they have been able to penetrate at all the mystery of this final act. What awaits him, and each of us, on the other side?

Several other revelations about the patient's immediate historical reality are equally disconcerting. The rift between parents and children, and the loneliness of the elderly are recurrent themes in Puiu's work. The first two ambulance "intermezzos" focus almost exclusively on the emotional distance between generations. Not much younger than her "client," Mioara shares his experience and woes. Both are disappointed with their offspring as are, one may guess, Leo's parents. Lazarescu has rechanneled his energy into caring for his cats, which are substitutes for the daughter who seems to have abandoned him (whether because he is a drunk and, therefore, unpleasant to be around, as his sister tells him on the phone, or because, as Sandu suggests, she is just heartless; or, probably, for any other number of reasons, especially economic). That he constantly thinks of her becomes evident later in the film, when, as he is losing consciousness, he mumbles something about spending Christmas with her. His solitude, as that of many parents, is not one of choice.

Mioara is in a similar situation. Her son lives with a woman out of wedlock, and she suffers for not being able to visit her granddaughter as she wishes. When Leo reveals that his brother has immigrated to Germany and that he has divorced his wife, Mioara comments, "You're such a messed-up generation." Mioara and Lazarescu, as well as Sandu and Miki, belong to the old world, in which marriages, good or bad, endured and the elders belonged in, and often guided, if not dominated, their children's lives (her last name, Avram, or the Romanian equivalent of Abraham, indicates her faith in a father-centered, cohesive world). Postcommunism, globalization, and the circulation of cultural practices dealt an unexpected blow to the unity of the nuclear family, and, by mid-2000s, the Ovidius of the 1990s had left the country. Children's freedom and parents' loneliness came hand in hand.

By the end of the film, individuals live in their own worlds. In one revealing scene, Lazarescu asks for water, Mioara complains about her liver pain, and Leo laments the fate of the driver involved in the accident. Within the small space of the van, the doctor's office, the hospital, or the city, people talk a lot but do not listen or hear each other. With few exceptions, there is no malice intended; they are simply too busy and self-preoccupied to see those around. The death of others is not an event for them.

Puiu has, nevertheless, made the death of Mr. Lazarescu an event for the viewer, encouraging empathy with the protagonist, in spite of his grumpiness, both at the narrative level and through aesthetic choices. The film has often been described as a comedy drama or a dark comedy, and it is fair to notice that the absurdity and humor hidden in many of

Figure 9: On the Styx

the situations can only further inspire viewers' responsiveness to Lazarescu's fate. Puiu is Eugène Ionesco's worthy offspring, in this respect. It is absurd that the protagonist's intellectual capacities deteriorate into aphasia and mental incoherence; or that the alcohol he ingests would also be used to sterilize his shaven head before surgery; or that somebody with the sonorous name of Lazarescu would stand no chance at resurrection (Quandt 81; Brooke 68). Visual puns are equally ironic: the round "cave" of the washing machine in the protagonist's kitchen prefigures the round "cave" of the CAT scanner later on, suggesting the regression of the brain as memory and language are washed away. The same shape also represents the scrutinizing eye of the camera, or that of the non-diegetic observers. A similarly expressive connection is made to the word "drill": the banal object a young neighbor borrows is, later on, compared to a surgeon's instrument by a brash young doctor. This drilling away at the same patient's consciousness and identity becomes the very object of viewers' study.

The humor only completes the picture: dark, often cruel jokes are part of the fiber of Lazarescu's world, and reflect its detached acceptance of death. "People should send you to fetch Death," sighs a bored Sandu when his wife delays bringing Lazarescu a glass of water. The protagonist himself makes time for a few bitter jokes. When Mioara asks him whether she can smoke, he answers that everything is allowed,

"Smoking, drinking. All the sins." Humor is a source of resistance and endurance, transforming an otherwise grim situation into an occasion for contemplation. The death of others becomes, imperceptibly, very close to home.

Mr. Lazarescu was hailed as a "hyperrealist fiction" or a "tour de force, with Puiu successfully simulating—or rather, orchestrating—the institutional texture of a Frederick Wiseman *vérité*" (Péron; Hoberman 232). It premiered on September 22, 2005 in Romania, with some audience success. Watched by around 30,000 domestic viewers, the film generated a controversy in the media when the Filmmakers' Union did not award it the Grand Prize (Radu 151; Șerban 27; Sava, *O istorie*, vol. 2: 116, 122).[28] Although it did not win the trophy of the 2005 Transylvania International Film Festival (TIFF), either, *Mr. Lazarescu* dominated the event, fueling discussions about the resistance of the establishment to the rise of a new form of cinema (Sava, *O istorie*, vol. 2: 120).[29] Ranking tenth on a list of the most important Romanian films between 1997 and 2009, the film failed to cover its costs and will, probably, become the property of the NCC in 2016 (Radu 151). Most of its earnings came from its international release, which was to become an eye-opener for the young Romanian directors ("The Death of Mr. Lazarescu"). A global stage meant increased competition, but also, for small nations and film industries, the chance for an art cinema to develop. Puiu understood the situation and would take advantage of it with his next film.

Author! Author! *Aurora*

The post-2006 years were important to the restructuring of the NCC and the revision of its policies. In January 2007, Puiu organized a press conference to analyze the Center's most recent actions. In December 2006, both his and Rădulescu's scripts had been rejected and, although a few other NRC representatives had received funding, most of the money, Puiu indicated, had been directed to dubious films with few chances of being made (Sava, *O istorie*, vol. 3: 239). What was more important, he argued, was that the Center lacked a cultural policy and its competition was the direct expression of the "restoration of mediocracy" (Sava, *O istorie*, vol. 3: 239). Puiu's position was supported by fifteen film critics, who signed an open letter attacking the criteria and procedures according to which the committee had chosen the winning projects (Sava, *O istorie,* vol. 3: 265).

The NCC seemed to adopt measures that would ensure the impartiality of the funding; in practice, very little changed. In 2008, Porumboiu and Puiu were allocated important sums of money for *Police, Adjective* and *Aurora,* respectively. As director Radu Muntean observed, the NCC was merely engaging in "criminal demagoguery" because the rest of the money was distributed to its perennial clients and to those with governmental connections (Sava, *O istorie,* vol. 3: 281–82). The situation escalated in 2009 when, after having been the member of the selection committee for a session, Mungiu wrote a scathing open letter to the Minister of Culture, exposing the deeply ingrained corruption of the system (Sava, *O istorie,* vol. 3: 292–95).

Romania's 2007 entry into the EU added an extra, decisive player to the game. Romanian directors were now able to apply for the MEDIA (Measures to Encourage the Development of the Audio Visual Industries) Program, an initiative intended to fund the production and distribution of European films ("MEDIA Programme"). EURIMAGES continued to be tremendously helpful, having financed not only the production but also the distribution and exhibition of NRC features ("Funding History"). The forging of a common European identity for many of the films that have been produced since 2007 is a reality: in terms of production and distribution, part of the national cinema is first European and then Romanian.

Aurora is a case in point. Only approximately 30 percent of the total cost of the film was supported by the NCC; the rest was financed by production companies from Romania, Switzerland, Germany, and France ("Concurs proiecte cinematografice"; Blaga, "*Aurora* Winds up Postproduction"). Furthermore, most of the film's distributors had received funding through either the EURIMAGES or the MEDIA programs ("Distribution Support—year 2010"; "Aurora"). *Aurora* was a European affair, but it could not have been able to gather the necessary capital without the endorsement of the NCC.

Is NRC more "European" than the rest of the local cinema (not directly supported through EU funding)? Opinions are divided. The Romanian public often rejects NRC films as sellouts, arguing that they depict what is worst about the nation because that is what is "exotic" to a (Western) European viewer, and it is this "other" viewer that supports their production.[30] This is a rather cynical perspective, which assumes that an individual's creative process is always targeted toward profit. In this assumption, however, there is a certain fear that, seen from the other's perspective, Romanians fall short, that they may be judged as less than "European," and that the divide between the two Europes still stands. From the perspective of the (Western) viewer, these films are, as Thomas Elsaesser argues, "post-national," in that they have the ability for "self-othering"; that is, they develop identities that are not so specific that they become impenetrable to a foreign audience (70–72). Furthermore, they simultaneously reflect on the process through which these identities are constructed and assumed (Elsaesser 70–72; Bardan 141–42). This may or may not be completely true. Even if films such as *Aurora,* Muntean's *Tuesday, After Christmas,* or Porumboiu's *Când se lasă seara peste București sau Metabolism* (When Evening Falls on Bucharest or Metabolism; 2013) seem to exist in a Bucharest as specific as the Berlin of *Lola rennt* (Run Lola Run; 1998), they remain profoundly anchored in a local reality and history that often escapes the foreign eye; they are less "post-national" than they may seem.

Aurora, Puiu's second feature in his projected Bucharest series, is the chronicle of a son who struggles with identity in a postpaternalistic society. He violently attempts to take on the father's role to preserve untouched his illusions about the past. The antihero conceives of himself as a savior, imposing his own set of moral rules in a world that, to him, has lost its compass (see also Pop 99). The film was inspired by readings in classics such as Fyodor Dostoyevsky's *Crime and Punishment,* Ernesto Sábato's *The Tunnel,* and Albert Camus's *The Stranger,* as well as films such as René Allio's *Moi, Pierre Rivière, ayant égorgé ma mere, ma soeur, et mon frère . . .* (I, Pierre Rivière; 1976) and a documentary series on Romanian television that included confessions of imprisoned murderers. Puiu also conducted interviews with various inmates (Puiu, "Cristi Puiu"; "An Interview" 10). Captivating in its study of a disturbed individual, *Aurora* is an intricate inquiry into the making of a "father," as well as into the tools and texts that constitute an author.

Viorel is a middle-aged loner who works in a factory and, for thirty-six hours, seems to wander about with no specific purpose other than to stalk and kill people. He spends his day at work and his evening with Gina

(Clara Vodă), one of the doctors in *Mr. Lazarescu,* and her daughter. The following morning, on the outskirts of the city, he stalks a young woman and then goes to work, where he fights with one colleague over money and retrieves a few illicitly made bullets from another one. He goes to a supermarket, following the same young woman he saw in the morning, and then arrives home, where he eats a bit, checks a rifle, takes a shower, and goes to talk with his upstairs neighbors about the water stain on his bathroom ceiling. Viorel is visited by Pușa (Valeria Seciu), his stepmother, and Doru (Valentin Popescu), her partner, who gives him advice about repainting the apartment. Once they leave, he gets dressed and, after withdrawing some money from an ATM and watching people from his car, he ends up at a weapons store. With a new gun, he goes to a cafeteria and then returns home only to find Dan (Gelu Colceag), his ex–father-in-law, taking some of the furniture from the apartment. The upstairs neighbor and his young son come to apologize for the stain and, once everybody leaves, Viorel tries out the new rifle and watches TV for a while. Eventually, he drives to the parking lot of a hotel, where he shoots a young couple. Back home, he packs three suitcases and, after a brief visit to Gina, who gives him a few sedative pills, he deposits his belongings at Pușa's, in his own childhood room. He returns to his apartment only to leave again at dawn and stalk the same young woman. Once she goes to work, he enters her house and kills Rodica (Catrinel Dumitrescu), an older woman who turns out to be his ex–mother-in-law; he then waits for her husband and kills him, too. Back in the city, he harasses a few women in a store, and then picks up his elder daughter from school to take her to Pușa's. His stepmother is not at home, however, so he leaves the girl with her neighbor, Mioara (Luminița Gheorgiu). In the end, Viorel surrenders to the police, confessing that he has killed his ex-wife's notary, whom he suspected to be her lover, the unknown woman who happened to be with him, and his ex–in-laws because they were responsible for his divorce.

Three hours long, *Aurora* may be frustrating in its slow pace and constant undermining of spectatorial expectations. Its exaggerated attention to inconsequential behavior may lead viewers astray, and its "mystery" seems, eventually, too mundane for the meticulous care with which it is built. Nevertheless, the film is prolific in its symbolism and offers a complex, multilayered gaze at an individual in crisis by means of several intersecting discourses (on the conflictual relationships within a brand new capitalist world, the inner workings of a man's psyche, and the makings of an auteur).

In spite of its universal themes, Puiu's film is very well anchored in a specific postcommunist reality and can be read as symptomatic of the new relationships established among various social classes in 2000s Romania. I suggest that, sociopolitically, Viorel is a "redundant male," resistant to change and adamant about recovering what he believes to be his rights and privileges (Mazierska 29). His direct attacks on others are generated by his frustration with what he perceives as their longtime, insidious undermining of his authority. Discussing the different forms of violence from a Marxist perspective, Slavoj Žižek argues that the systemic, long-engrained, outreaching violence associated with the workings of capitalism is so pervasive that it is almost invisible, constituting the "zero-level standard" against which any other aggression is measured (2). There are two visible expressions of this "objective" violence: "symbolic violence," which may surface in all discourses (cinema included), and "subjective violence," the apparently irrational, direct violence that appears out of nowhere, but is, in fact, only the means through which the pressure accumulated within the system erupts (Žižek 10–11). Viorel's "subjective" violence is an expression of his accumulated grievances with a world that has marginalized him, both economically and politically; his ex–in-laws are merely its latest agents.

By 2009, Romania's economic growth, probably the fastest in Europe at the time, had reached its peak and, with it, so did consumerism (Gledhill and King 324). Salaries rose, the infrastructure improved, and companies thrived. Real estate became more accessible, in spite of its increasing cost, so gated communities developed especially around the busiest cities, giving birth to entrepreneurial suburbanites. This new class was more globally mobile and sought to rearrange the relationships within the system in order to fit in. In the process, the more reluctant to change an agent was, the more likely it would be to succumb and be replaced. It is against this new world and its individualism that Viorel becomes violent.

That the protagonist belongs to a dying world is most evident in Pușa's apartment, the only one that he recognizes as his home. Heavy, solid, sculpted furniture, ancient photos and paintings of natural landscapes, shelves of books and LPs, Asian vases, China statuettes and exotic lampshades, old, silver candle sticks, framed collections of rocks, and antlers, all adorn this house, populating it with the memories of long-gone eras. Though the furniture is difficult to trace to a precommunist era, some of the photographs are not (especially one, oval in form, of a male ancestor). These objects belong to a family with a history, and the resources and cultural background to preserve it. Viorel's ancestors were, probably, members of the pre-1945 bourgeoisie. His room similarly bursts with old furniture, books, ELO and Led Zeppelin posters, all indices of a comfortable life in the 1970s and 1980s. This apartment, located in one of the precommunist buildings in Bucharest, contains, therefore, a rather strange story of a prewar middle-class family (possibly belonging to the intelligentsia) who continued to enjoy a relative prosperity during communism. Such a case would have been rare. In the late 1940s and early 1950s, the communists conducted widespread campaigns against those deemed bourgeois, who were largely dispossessed and thrown in jail (Deletant 84–89).

Further clues are also "visible" only to Romanian and, possibly, Eastern European viewers. That Viorel did have a rather privileged childhood is subtly indicated through a few objects, all of which did not belong to the economy of communist Romania, but were brought into the country by those who could travel or had relatives abroad: the toy cars (very prized possessions among boys at the time); the model ship that Viorel places on a top shelf; and the little model plane he lays on top of a few books. Two other objects may help experienced viewers understand the family history: the antlers and the old rifle Viorel brings back home. The communist regime controlled weapon possession and foreign travel very tightly, and it is highly unlikely that a representative of the former bourgeoisie would have been granted the right to own a firearm AND to travel abroad (or have communication with Western countries). Puiu identifies Viorel's father as a member of the Securitate, a "hunter" in a very real sense of the word. I would add that the film text also suggests that the family must hide a betrayal, a pact with the devil that allowed it to preserve its middle-class history almost intact. *Aurora* is thus very much a film of its moment, which engages directly with the moral failings of the 2006 official condemnation of communism in Romania.[31]

Viorel is the last descendant of this old world, even if, to a (Western) European audience he may appear as any other member of the postindustrial middle classes. His most prized possessions are the LPs, CDs, and DVDs (or the memories) he has accumulated (he is concerned that the movers do not take them). The upright piano in his girls' room hints at his desire to pass on his heritage. A "specialist consultant in metallurgical engineering," he is one of the many engineers "produced" on a large scale to supply personnel for a heavy industry that was to die an agonizing death after 1989. Unlike Lazarescu, Viorel is still too young to retire, and he has found a job in one of the few factories still alive in the 2000s. His coworkers, however, seem to sabotage him, and his income is not high enough to allow him to preserve the rather privileged status his father once ensured his family. Viorel lives in a two-bedroom apartment, in a building where manual laborers like his neighbor can also afford a home. These are the new precariat classes: people with different degrees of education (there is a world of difference between him, or Gina for that matter, and his neighbors), with very different family histories, whose status is defined by income and insecurity. It is a change that leaves him nostalgic for the safety of his childhood world, all the more so when his job is under threat, too.

In her discussion of the dominant types of male characters in Polish postcommunist cinema, Ewa Mazierska notes that, as a result of profound socioeconomic changes, men's roles as patriarchs and Romantic heroic figures came under threat (29–32). In cinema, the result of this crisis was the rise of the "redundant male," whose virility and potential, when they exist, can no longer find the space for expression in a society where women are increasingly gaining visibility and sociopolitical power (37–39). In Romania, postcommunist disillusionment and the rapid rise of the precariat classes have led to the birth of the antihero in the NRC. Doru Pop suggests that such characters represented a "double folded rejection" of two male figures—the Hollywood and the communist (action) heroes—and are, therefore, subversive models (87). Viorel, he also argues, is even a step further removed, as he is "profoundly antisocial and amoral," without any justification for his behavior (99). Puiu's antihero is, I propose, a "redundant male," whose nostalgia for a patriarchal world of male privilege becomes extreme in the aftermath of his divorce. He is not amoral, but morally outdated and radical in his views, and his impotence and misunderstanding of women only aggravate his condition. Viorel is a deposed father, who feels trapped in a present he does not understand and, therefore, seeks to erase.

Pușa's neighbors are also likely to be the victims of the new order, but in a different way than Viorel. Mioara, the nurse who cared for Lazarescu, appears to be the sole breadwinner in the house; her husband, old and sickly looking, is probably retired. They were, conceivably, assigned this apartment by the communist regime, in one of its dashing moves to repopulate the houses confiscated from the bourgeoisie with the new urbanites coming to study and work in the city. Mioara's furniture is old, but dates back only to the socialist production system. The many paintings of flowers adorning the walls suggest the family's desire to pass for middle class in communism and afterward. The nephew who wants to convince them to replace their kitchen furniture, and the son who, nonchalantly, engages in amorous relations right under his parents' noses, are signs that Mioara's universe (of waning patriarchy) is as much under threat as Viorel's.

Rodica and Dan Livinski, the in-laws, are the winners of the new age; they are the "new class." If Viorel appreciates the intangible (music, memory, childhood), they value accumulation and let nothing go to waste, not even the furniture that their daughter gained in the divorce and for which they have no more space in their home. They live in a former village now slowly turning into suburbia. Big, brand new, and dull, their house is surrounded by a metal fence that protects it from prodding eyes as if it were a fortress. The piano they take from Viorel is an odd stand-alone piece in a living room crammed to the ceiling with panel-made, Ikea-like furniture. The aura of the old objects in Pușa's apartment is in striking contrast to the blandness of these mechanically reproduced shelves, couches, chairs, and tables. The windows surrounding the kitchen and separating it from the living room give viewers the impression of a greenhouse, especially when the camera is situated in the house foyer. This is an insulated world, smugly satisfied with its status, and little interested in contact with others. They are the new capital, and theirs is the economic and political power Viorel's father once enjoyed.

The protagonist's in-laws have merely risen with the tide. Elsewhere in Bucharest, young women find good jobs in the government because their age and beauty helps them (as does the mysterious Andreea, possibly a friend of Viorel's wife); telecommunication cables stretch like cobwebs everywhere; and glass buildings take over huge spaces of the city, forcing older architecture into their shadows. Outside the Livinskis' home, huge trucks and trailers are parked on a vacant lot, deep in mud, yet ready for the road. This is a world of transactions, in which everything is up to be exchanged. It pushes out people like Mioara and Gina, whose work does not produce capital, and Viorel, whose exactitude and patriarchal moral sense do not serve its interests. The protagonist's execution of the notary public and his *nouveaux-riches* in-laws is, therefore, a form of subjective violence, a singular act of revenge that appears disproportionate and nonsensical, but that expresses the frustrations and animosities of those left behind by the "brand new world." It is the act of an individual who cannot stop time, but who wants to regain control of his own small universe.

The prologue paints the picture of a solitary man, confined within rigid structures, and conflicted between action and nonaction. The opening long shot of a dead-end inner courtyard of a factory, half occluded by a wall, reveals two characters: one disappears behind a building, while the other, Viorel, smokes feverishly and paces around. The straight angles and parallel lines of the building shapes and the grids that dominate this shot are echoed by those in the next one, from inside the industrial plant, where huge cylinders dominate the foreground while rectangles, diagonal railings, and horizontal wall paneling mark the background. This rather geometric *mise en scène* is the backdrop for Viorel's apparently belligerent discussion with a coworker, completely silenced by the sounds of machines. The setting for the third shot is a second, derelict factory courtyard, where V-shaped girders, abandoned concrete blocks, an industrial conveyor belt, and massive metal containers confine the character, as if within a cage. Carrying a green folder in hand, he leaves, changes his mind, and turns around, going in the opposite direction. If prologues give any hints about the plot, not much is revealed in this one. Viorel is a taciturn man, with fraught relationships at work, and seemingly caught in a bind; his movements are indecisive and he appears to bear a secret within the covers of the folder. The aura of mystery that surrounds the protagonist will not dissipate even after his confession in the end. As the title suggests ("aurora" translates as "dawn/sunrise" in Romanian), any representation of one's motives and actions is necessar-

Figure 10: Trapped |

ily ambiguous, incomplete, and only a beginning. In this sense, Puiu is challenging previous texts—he directly refers to F. W. Murnau's *Sunrise* (1927)—for their moral and narrative clarity ("Interview").

The director's thoughts regarding Viorel's intentions have gained in nuance over time. In a 2011 interview, he noted that, "[Viorel] is distressed. He already took the decision to kill before the beginning of the film. He already has the rifle and is already in the mood to kill"; nevertheless, he could not have changed completely, so the intention is to show that "a criminal is like everybody else" ("Interview"). A year later, Puiu comments further on his protagonist's behavior, "Some people say Viorel *is* autistic—I don't agree. If you take this extreme decision—to kill—you don't seek dialogue. You are on a completely different track" ("Murder in Mind" 42). He added that, in spite of his decision, Viorel's reactions are unpredictable, "The dynamic of our existence is not so easy to decode. . . . So I said, 'Yes, he wants to kill this notary because he thinks he's his wife's lover'—and then the act of killing changes him. It frees something inside him" (Puiu, "Murder in Mind" 42). I would suggest that any interpretation of the film needs to take into consideration two sets of viewers: the first- and the second-time. Many of the character's actions may appear unpredictable and random to a first-time spectator, but, upon repeated screenings, they indicate his edgy rapport with others. Yes, in unimportant matters, Viorel is like everybody else:

he eats, takes showers, buys food and shaving foam in supermarkets, and watches TV late at night. Largely responsible for this impression is Puiu's treatment of time and plot, reminiscent of films such as Agnés Varda's *Cléo de 5 à 7* (Cleo from 5 to 7; 1962) or Chantal Akerman's *Jeanne Dielman, 23 Quai du Commerce, 1080 Bruxelles* (1983), in that the organizing principle seems to be "a day in the life of." Slow, tedious moments take as much, if not more, narrative space than more significant ones. At a much deeper level, however, he is qualitatively different, and this becomes visible only upon a second viewing.

Puiu's use of tropes of the thriller genre further constructs first-time viewers' expectations in particular ways. The most obvious is the presence of the rifle that will, indeed, be fired (even if against unknown people and for unknown reasons). Once Viorel kills his initial victims, one cannot but become highly suspicious of everything else he does. Although the second round of murders comes late, it does come; the first-time viewers' apprehension, therefore, colors their perception for the remaining two thirds of the film. The antihero's journey thus combines possible sources for his apparent discontent with everyday, emotionally neutral actions, and making the difference between them becomes increasingly difficult for all types of viewers.

Aurora is another account of an unsuccessful initiation, as was the case with *Stuff and Dough* and *Mr. Lazarescu*. It is only in light of Viorel's confession that, upon a second viewing, one may make sense of—that is, impose one's own meaning on—the events. The antihero imposes his own "order" in the world and achieves the status of father, surrendering himself in the end on his own terms. His initiation as a patriarch fails only in that he aligns himself with the forces of evil and becomes a malefic "savior."

A web of obscure relationships organizes Viorel's everyday life. The first scene is set at Gina's, in the evening, as her daughter is going to bed. The man is in a dark room, smoking and looking outside the window; when the girl (Ileana Puiu, Cristi Puiu's daughter) claims the mother's attention, he walks slowly toward the doorway, peeking outside at the interaction between the two. He is a prowler in the dark, moving noiselessly and observing others in silence. That Viorel may be a hunter on the loose is further suggested in the discussion he and Gina soon have in the kitchen. She recounts her daughter's observation that, when the hunter in *Little Red Riding Hood* cuts open the wolf's belly, the grandmother should come out naked because the predator is wearing her clothes. In adopting Charles Perrault's fairy tale as one of its subtexts, the film places the issue of putting on and taking off identities at its core; it also signals the director's interest in establishing a relationship between the profane and the sacred dimensions of life. Viorel is a "hunter": he watches everybody, works on one rifle and then buys another, and, eventually, shoots those he considers "wolves" in disguise. By the end, however, he also turns out to be a wolf himself: he is constantly changing clothes, and stalks his daughters' "grannie" only to do away with her. The two little girls in the film—Gina's daughter and Lumi (Carmela Culda), Viorel's child—have similar red boots and telling attitudes toward the antihero: one dismisses and the other trusts him; both are blind to the possible danger he may pose (if not to them, then to others).

The first part of the narrative, however, keeps Viorel's nefarious instincts at bay and turns the spotlight on his other, more vulnerable social persona. He appears to be everybody's victim. The casual deli vendor does not give him the right change; drivers block him in traffic or are inconsiderate; and people take their time at ATMs or in cafeterias, completely oblivious to those, like the protagonist, waiting their turn. More notably, his coworkers seem to have plotted against him, while Doru and Dan deride his efforts to refurbish his apartment.

Puiu relies, again, on thick description to construct a complex, almost impenetrable world. Viorel is a stickler for small details and too sensitive about the ways in which the others relate to him. In all cases, he is not wrong in what he believes—people do seem careless and self-centered—but only in the degree to which he adheres to very rigid moral expectations and the extent to which he refuses to compromise. Puiu describes him as a man with a deficient understanding of fairy tales, who considers it his mission to restore the "balance" of things. He expects society to function according to his own strict rules and seeks justice in the Name of the Father.

Viorel's biological father is dead, and he contests and dismisses all those who attempt to impose their authority on him. Doru, Pușa's partner, is the more benign figure. A rather flabby, unattractive man, slightly older than Viorel but, probably, younger than his consort, he puffs out his chest and criticizes the tools and materials the protagonist is using to renovate the apartment. Dressed in a black, elegant coat that does not suit him, he goes from room to room and repeats his advice as if addressing a child. Upon leaving, he tries to make a joke, "We came, in fact, because we thought you were not at home and we wanted to fool around." Viorel disdains Doru's veiled attack on his manliness and sexual innuendos, and he is not content with Pușa, either (whose tender gestures he constantly rejects). He, nevertheless, lets her take care of him (she washes and irons his clothes) and gives her instructions to keep his room locked. There is a certain intimacy between the two that becomes evident when Pușa, puzzled by Doru's moping around in the kitchen, confesses to Viorel, "He behaves like a pregnant woman." Doru is an intruder, yet not one to pose a real threat, and both Pușa and Viorel know it.

The other, more abrasive male figure is Dan, the protagonist's ex–father-in-law, who echoes Doru's critical comments when he comes to collect the furniture granted to his daughter as a result of the divorce. A short, stout man who wears glasses and tends to keep his hands clasped behind his back, Dan watches Viorel intensely; he is placed in the same position as the camera in one of the first shots of this sequence. He is the incontestable *pater familias,* and his visit is only one more opportunity to discipline his ex–son-in-law. Dan is the authentic usurper of the Father position, so the unstable protagonist might well think that eliminating this man would restore him to his rightful status within the family.

That Viorel is at a crossroads becomes evident from the appearance of his apartment. One in-depth shot reveals three rooms in three stages of transformation. The closest to the viewer is what used to be the daughters' room, with its walls still covered in old wallpaper, whose pattern of little houses, trees, and cars bears the marks of little fingers and years of family life. The hallway is bare of furniture, and its scraped walls bleed cords, sockets, and switches, which indicate the discomfort and pain of a transitory phase; this is the space where Viorel is confronted by two detested "fathers," Doru and Dan. Finally, the distant kitchen, all tiled in white, with a white table, white stools, and white cabinets, emanates the smell of sanitizers one associates with hospital rooms. This is the aseptic future the protagonist may have in mind, but which seems constantly invaded by others (his stepmother, Doru, Dan, or a mysterious feminine voice on the phone). In between a distressing past

Figure 11: At crossroads

and a sterilized future, the antihero bides his time watching others and checking if anybody is following him.

Four women populate Viorel's world. Amalia, his wife, is seen from a distance, when he is stalking her: a young, pretty woman, she appears demure with her rather long, old-fashioned skirt and dull jacket. The antihero describes her as a child, inexperienced and too trusting of people; in his eyes, she is the gullible prey of a sexual predator such as the notary public. Viorel has no moral qualms about killing his supposed rival, even if it implies shooting a second, unknown and innocent person. This man who demands absolute moral integrity from everybody around him does not think twice about this extra victim, which denotes his desperate, self-centered urge to take control of those around.

Although he is involved with Gina, Viorel does not consider her an adequate partner; she is the other woman. Interestingly, in the version released at the 2010 Cannes Film Festival, the prologue was a medium shot of Viorel and Gina in bed, naked. Although it is difficult to distinguish the two faces because the scene is set at night, one can hear Gina sobbing; she then gets up and goes to the bathroom. The final version of the film completely omits (one might say represses) this moment that signaled Viorel's inability to connect with this woman (and, possibly, his impotence). The only information that is preserved is that, though slightly more sexualized (after all, she is the only woman in the film to engage the voyeur in the viewer when she slowly rolls up her stockings in the opening scene), Gina is, ultimately, a turnoff. She is an overworked single mother with a hectic schedule, and not fully trustworthy because she is not able to deliver on what she promises. Furthermore, she treats Viorel too much as a second child—especially notable in her use of diminutives and controlling tone of voice—for him to be comfortable with her. Puiu considers that the actress changed the role he had envisioned for this character (he wanted Gina to be the ideal partner whom Viorel fails to acknowledge because of his tunnel vision). As she appears in the film, however, this woman is too independent and self-possessed not to be a threat to Viorel's archaic vision of family.

Pușa, his stepmother, is an equally challenging figure. Her soft touch, affectionate words, and constant care for him suggest a well-established relationship. She has a fine intuition about this grown-up man (she tells him he has a fever when, indeed, he has been feverishly preparing for the murders) and she is neither shy nor afraid to let him know what she thinks. She is the one who keeps the rituals associated with the dead. When commemorating a departed family member, one is advised to share food with others; the food, blessed by a priest, takes on symbolical signification in that it is believed that it is offered directly to the dead. Pușa returns from the commemoration of Viorel's father and offers him such blessed food, scolding him for having skipped the event. Viorel takes it mechanically, fully missing its value as a reminder of the world beyond and, implicitly, of one's mortality. The antihero fails to recognize the need to be humble. He only tolerates Pușa because he perceives her as a vestige of a previous life he idealizes.

Dan's wife, Rodica is the other face of the "mother." Like Pușa, she pays attention to Viorel's state of mind and body, and she is equally intuitive about him: "You look tired. Why aren't you sleeping?" she asks.[32] Women are, in Puiu's films, much more perceptive about those around them, and more attuned to, even if less assertive about, the presence of the sacred, be it in its benign or malefic forms. Rodica scolds Viorel for his detailed calculation of how much they had helped each other in the past. The scene is filmed from a medium distance by a fixed camera that pays close attention both to his increasing tenseness and to her meticulous movements while cutting some potatoes. Each of her gestures is doubled by reproaches, which only amplify the protagonist's ire. He follows and pummels her to death. This physical, carnal contact with the mother figure is an expression of his sexual frustration and anger. When he comes back to shoot her, he steps carefully in between her legs, pointing the long barrel of the rifle at the body; after a few hesitating seconds, when he moves a few steps back, regroups, steps forward, and shoots; smoke trickles out of the gun. The bullet's penetration of the woman's body is an act of rape through which Viorel symbolically regains his sexual, as well as social and political potency; it is the origin of his own new world.[33] The killing of the father (-in-law) is next, and the "hunter" waits for him patiently, his hand resting on the rifle barrel. He has now become more of a man than before, the founder of a new order.

The two sets of murders isolate the second part of the narrative, one that obsessively points toward Viorel's childhood as a possibly contradictory site of both comfort and frustration. This prolonged withdrawal into memory is prefaced, in the first part of the film, by the protagonist's relationship with his upstairs neighbors. Having just returned from a long night out, he is taking a shower when he notices that the ceiling has been flooded. In the next shot, he watches a young mother scolding and throwing toys at her son. The scene is visually memorable for its immaculate, almost unreal whiteness: of the walls in the neighbor's apartment; of Viorel's long-sleeve shirt; and, as he goes downstairs, of the hallway and the light coming through the windows. The "flood" is one of memory and the protagonist seems to identify with the little boy, to whom he extends a helping hand. A few hours later, when the boy's father publicly chastises him, Viorel is more understanding of the situation; it is, the film suggests, a possible *déja-vu* for him.

After the first murders, the protagonist dives even more into his past. In one scene, he carefully packs his toy cars into an Ikea box; later he takes them, together with three other suitcases full of LPs, CDs, and books, to Pușa's and stores them in his childhood bedroom. Although not predictable, his actions seem to be in preparation for another event (even for first-time viewers who cannot guess this "event"). After a few more trips, he returns home, goes into the basement of the building, to his storage room, and takes out a radiator. Central in this crammed space is a little sled, a possible hint at Viorel's "Rosebud" memories. Visually and symbolically, his descent in search of a source of heat may indicate his craving for the past as a space of safety, in spite of the possible conflicts it may have harbored as well. Eventually, he brings the radiator into the kitchen and sets it by the side of his two bags (one that contains the rifle). The past (the radiator), present (the bags), and future (the kitchen) coexist in one moment, as the film text indicates their interdependence and relevance to the character's actions. Viorel looks to each side and then he seems to stare toward the camera (positioned across the hallway, in the girls' former bedroom).

Puiu explains the intention behind the camera-observer:

> The only valid pointer I gave the people behind the camera was: "*the camera's gaze should be that of a parent looking at his child who has just learned to walk. . . .*" I told them, "*His father died long ago, he is in heaven, he is looking at his child and he sees how he is moving toward perdition, but he cannot intervene.*" And every time I was in front of the camera, in my mind I went back to the people who have vanished from my life. I sought to enter a dialogue with them, to hear them, in fact. ("An Interview" 13)

The director is very precise about his own thoughts while playing the character: "I thought of my father, who was dead, I thought of my grandfather, who was dead, of myself as a child in my relationship with these people who were dead and who were close to me in the past. And who had vanished from my memory because I go back to them more and more rarely" ("An Interview" 13). If the camera is to look at Viorel as

Figure 12: In search of the Father |

a father looking at his child, and if Viorel/Puiu is to think of his dead father, then we may safely assume that this physically absent, yet constantly present observer is nothing other than the Ghost of the Father. Viorel senses this presence—hence his frequent peeking through his apartment windows or the door's peephole—but he cannot completely grasp it, nor comprehend its nature. He never fully acknowledges it (there is no direct glance into the camera), which suggests the failure of his initiation into the sacred.

Once his in-laws are dead, Viorel acquires the power and identity of a father, and is recognized by the others as such. This shortcut "crossing" into the status of a parent, however, implies the putting on of a new identity. His first trip is to a menswear store, but, before he enters, the film text legibly marks his new status: a long shot reveals the word "DÅD" written on the wall adjacent to the store window.[34] The word may be interpreted as an involuntary expression of the latent "content" of the narrative: Viorel appears as a new "father"; the film itself enacts the "deed" of becoming a father; but, in the process, he emerges as a "dead father," a "dead savior," one may add, whose reign begins and ends with his murderous acts.

No other character will scold or dismiss him from now on. In the third part, first-time viewers' apprehension reaches its peak, especially as the man himself becomes increasingly irascible and falters in self-control.

Figure 13: DÅD |

Traffic noise, whether from rail tracks, from the city streets, or even from within the factory, is always very loud and contrasts with the mood of the previous scenes. Viorel "moves" from the suburban house of his in-laws into the busy Bucharest thoroughfares; from the relative calm at his youngest daughter's kindergarten to the loud honking and noise of a busy intersection; and from the warm reception at Mioara's into the dangerous street, where he is caught between two passing trams. These repeated similar cuts give the impression that time is accelerating, and that the man is running out of breath. Again, Puiu frustrates expectations: not only does the antihero refrain from any other murder, but he also eventually turns himself in to the police.

All the new characters he meets recognize in him a determination that stops them in their tracks. The shop assistants find him peculiar, and they are somewhat apprehensive of this man who pushes them around. Surrounded by Valentino suits (who are to belong to "fathers" whose economic and political status Viorel would never attain), the protagonist forces the young women to acknowledge his authority. In the very next scene, a pensive Viorel is smoking while Dmitri Shostakovich's *Hamlet* (Puiu chose the sequence titled "Hunting") is heard on a radio, a subtle suggestion to his identity as the Hunter, an avenger of injustice, the idealized image that he may, unconsciously, have had of himself. In a subsequent scene, the protagonist yanks his elder daughter out of a rehearsal for a show, intimidating the teacher who has to give in to his authority. It is important to notice that, having murdered his in-laws, who would have been responsible for picking up his daughters, Viorel takes this responsibility upon himself, thereby asserting his newly gained status. Mioara, the neighbor who agrees to take care of the girl, also addresses him as a father before he even has the chance to introduce himself as such. "Is this one yours?" she asks, pointing to his daughter. Viorel displays all the "signs" of a father.

His surrender to the police is also done on his own terms in that he grants himself the authority to tell the story. The scene is revelatory in how little it does, in fact, disclose about this man. The white, vinyl bag he has been carrying, a visual metaphor, perhaps, for his unconscious burden, contains banal objects (the cheese pies he has just bought, the apple Gina gave him, his cap, and a highlighter). This scene is the appropriate culmination of a series of small gestures made by a man closed off, by choice, from all others. Viorel is reluctant to speak and keeps his eyes open to everything around him. The entire prologue is devoid of words, and he spends most of his time alone at home or journeying through the city. When he does speak, he merely responds to others and says very little to illuminate his actions, to a first- or second-time viewer. Even in this final confession, his longest speech yet, the antihero has difficulty in articulating a straightforward explanation of the events, but gives enough fragmentary details so that viewers, and the police, can reconstruct them. He is very precise about dates, places, and identities, but his cryptic pronouncements have to do with his effort to explain why he committed the murders: "I don't know what you think but I believe that the justice system cannot comprehend the level of complexity of the relationship I had with my wife" or, "Don't get me wrong, but I've been listening to you. You seem to think you understand. You seem to think you follow what I'm saying. And that scares me." These attempts, however, underscore his inability to verbalize even the part that he himself has acknowledged so far. Viorel's firm rejection of the chaos generated by desire and the violent imposition of his "order" have, in his eyes, earned him the status of father; he is, however, a fallen father, whose actions ruin his family. He turns himself in because he believes the police to be the embodiment of the Law, whose recognition he seeks. Viorel expects that writing down the events will grant him the acknowledgment he craves, but the act is to remain incomplete and incoherent.

This need to assert control is also at the heart of the third type of discourse embedded within the film: the question of authorship. The final scene is revelatory in this respect as it invites viewers to reconsider the entire narrative as a gradual revelation of the mind behind the camera. Having confessed and partially explained his deeds, Viorel awaits the decision of the two policemen. He is asked to write down his confession. "Can I have a pen?" he asks. To *cinéphiles,* the writing instrument, required by the director impersonating a character, is an oblique reference to Alexandre Astruc's famously coined phrase *camera-stylo,* the "camera-pen."[35] Astruc defined cinema as a language: "By language, I mean a form in which and by which an artist can express his thoughts, however abstract they may be, or translate his obsessions exactly as he does in the contemporary essay or novel" (Astruc qtd. in Williams 306).

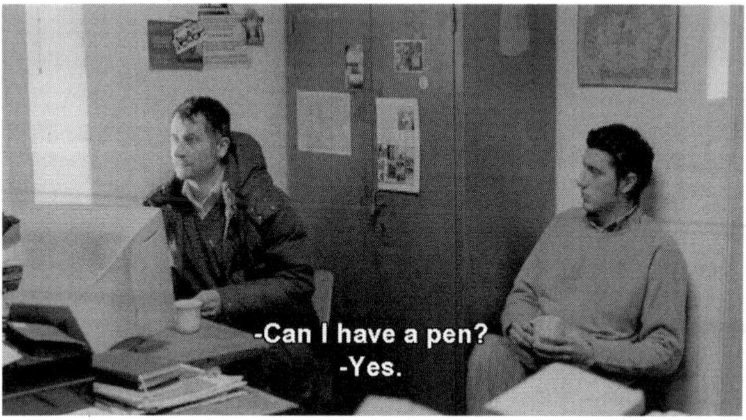

Figure 14: Can I have a pen? |

The last image of Viorel/Puiu about to (re-)write his "thoughts" and "obsessions" underscores the fate of an author, "condemned" to partial, incomplete, inexact knowledge and ability of expression.

The Romanian director further emphasizes this impossibility of omniscience and narrative closure when he compares the act of filmmaking to that of murder: " . . . [W]hether conscientiously or not, jurisprudence calls the murderer 'the author of the crime.' Author! Author! Author of the text, author of the painting. . . . They're contiguous. What the murderer does is to intervene brutally in the order of things, in our history"; he adds that an author also intervenes in history, "[e]xcept that his [or her] interventions in history are of the soft kind. Being a creator is a very dangerous thing" ("An Interview" 9). It implies fathering a new world. In *Aurora*, the "brutality" of the author's intervention is expressed in the relentless restriction of narration and point of view, and in the subtle winking at a world that escapes the frame.

Writing about the modes of organization of cinematic discourse, Seymour Chatman argues that there is a clear distinction between the "implied author" of a film, the one who "has invented it all" and, therefore, possesses absolute knowledge, and the "cinematic narrator" that merely "presents what the cinematic implied author requires" (478). This narrator is not to be restricted merely to a character or the camera from whose point of view a film may be constructed, but is to be understood as a complex system that consists of a "visual channel" (acting, cinematography, and editing are included here) and an "auditory channel" (type and origin of sound belong to this category) (Chatman 483). If, for Chatman, the "implied author" is the director who, in collaboration with others, holds the key to the text, for Puiu there is a higher agency that transcends the director and his crew, and has absolute knowledge. I would suggest that, according to his philosophy, a filmmaker merely channels the vision of a transcendental author into the actual text of the "cinematic narrator." The task of this physical author, whose experience and understanding of reality are limited, is to "resonate" with the world and be open to its different dimensions; such receptivity may lead one to catch the "ineffable" ("An Interview" 9, 10, 15). It is this transcendence that film and viewer may share. In *Aurora,* therefore, Puiu's purpose in constantly underscoring the limits of the cinematic narrator is to hint at the presence of a much more knowledgeable, transcendental, "implied" author.

Discussing the viewers' experience of watching a self-reflexive film, Vivian Sobchack argues that spectators can occupy three different positions: they can follow what the film depicts and perceive it as mediated and opaque; they can follow the "camera," that is, the immediately visible mediator, and have no conflicts about the object of the film; or they can "see [themselves] watching the film" and be, thus, detached from the film world (Sobchack 282–84). In *Aurora,* we see the camera seeing Viorel seeing the others. Although not self-reflexive in that it does not disclose itself directly as an act of fiction organized according to a set of rules (it does not break the fourth wall), Puiu's film is self-aware. We are once removed from Viorel's world and twice removed from what he sees, and this type of conceptual frame within frame only invokes the hidden "hand" responsible for such structuring. *Aurora* engages spectators in what I shall term "detached introspection": an attempt at configuring the character's inner world that is repeatedly hindered and that, therefore, draws attention to the film's own act of seeing.[36]

Such attention is achieved especially through the use of the camera-observer, and the limitation, and reframing, of its point of view. This important element of the cinematic narrator tends to place itself in a different space, removed from the "action," thus forcing the door or window frames within the film world to restrict spectators' view. The camera also refuses to move; it only pans or tilts, and in most cases, only shifts slightly. Furthermore, it seems obsessed with Viorel, focusing on him even when the interest may be in a different part of the profilmic space. When Pușa and Doru visit him, the camera, set in the daughters' room, does not follow Doru as he inspects and comments on what he sees. It also does not go into the kitchen with Pușa to "show" what she is doing, but focuses on Viorel as he passes back and forth in the hallway and finally sits down to put on his socks. There is one room in his apartment—his and his ex-wife's bedroom—that viewers never get to see, and one can imagine it as the site of the protagonist's trauma. The camera-observer becomes, especially in the final part of the film, increasingly emotional, relatively apprehensive of what Viorel is about to do. The most conspicuous example of its suspicion is its refusal to follow the antihero upstairs, where he beats his mother-in-law unconscious. This refusal goes against viewers' expectations, emphasizing their inability to see (and control) events.

This silent observer is particularly well positioned for one moment that reveals the film's self-awareness. Early in the plot, Viorel is cleaning a very old rifle. He points its barrel at the camera, and pulls the trigger. This virtual acknowledgment of the "watcher" and the act of "shooting" is troublesome to viewers, who themselves occupy the position of the camera. The "shooting" forces spectators to detach from the narrative, if only momentarily, and acknowledge it as the product of a higher agency that remains itself unscarred by the act. Puiu (the director) shoots himself (as Viorel) "shooting" himself/the viewers/the author; all are at risk.

A similar role is played by the scene in which Viorel takes a shower and checks his body. This moment is an expression of the human author's (the director's) "nakedness" in front of his spectators, in that it implies that he is about to expose the process of making a film, its limits, its "diseases," and "obsessions" in a manner that strips all voyeuristic pleasure, leaving viewers uncomfortable. Puiu's text constantly points to the existence of an author, yet one who is imperfect and vulnerable.

Probably the most revelatory scene is the final one. The reference to the *caméra-stylo* is not singular. Viorel asks to sit on a particular chair and, as he is confessing, the sunset light falls on his face. This natural "spotlight" places him (and the question of the author, implicitly) at the center of viewers' attention. It also represents an indirect

Figure 15: The shot I

citation of film noir thrillers. The Rosebud sled, the presence of "rear windows" that can be seen from Viorel's apartment, and, in one scene, the framing of train tracks to mimic the Lumière brothers' *L'Arivée d'un train en gare de La Ciotat* (The Arrival of a Train at La Ciotat Station; 1895) are further indicators that *Aurora* is a film that alludes to other films and the art of cinema. In our discussion, Puiu argued that these quotations became visible only during editing, and that he did not intend them in advance. Nevertheless, they appear as "proof" of the existence of a higher authority (the transcendental author) whose "signs" both director (that is, human author) and viewers can recognize only in retrospect.

What is an author, then? The debate surrounding *auteurs* emerged within the group of writers at the *Cahiers du Cinéma* after World War II. Peter Wollen argues that an author was perceived to exhibit similar interests and aesthetic preferences throughout the corpus of his or her films, even if these could vary, change, and be reinvented from one work to another (529). The filmmakers themselves, however, were separate entities from the structures that bore their names (Wollen 532). An *auteur* was, furthermore, "an unconscious catalyst" of all those involved in the making of each text (Wollen 532). There is, in Wollen's famous essay, an attempt to reduce the influence of one individual (the director as *auteur*) over the entire film not only in recognition of the team cooperation necessary for each production, but also as an acknowledgment that no individual could have complete control over his or her oeuvre.

By the 2000s, the author was no longer regarded as the ultimate source of the film, and had lost the authority over the interpretation of his or her work. Dudley Andrew emphasizes the disappearance of the *auteur* behind the text, from where it must be excavated by spectators (23). Although the international film market has invested *auteurism* with renewed importance, connected to the film's marketing, it has also transformed the author into a name (Andrew 23). Andrew points out, however, that, even if the author is an "effect" of "readers and text," there still endures a faith in the existence of an *auteur* whose experience is the source of the film (27).

Is the author dead? Take the example of Cristi Puiu. The present essay, set in dialogue with the interview of the director, suggests that an author is born at the intersection between the viewers' and the director's experience of a body of work, an experience necessarily limited, incomplete, and grounded in each side's particular exposure to, and understanding of, the world (Sobchack 260). But these texts are not the only ones. There are the other texts, of the actors and the crew, the producers, and the distributors. There is the text of the market, which turns the author into a brand, easily or not so easily produced, promoted, and sold. And there is the text of the film festival circuit, of utmost importance to directors like Puiu coming from a small national film industry. Texts keep multiplying: the texts of academia and cinema magazines, or those of glossy covers, zealous promoters, and fans. Authorship seems to have become a shared endeavor. At its core, however, responsible for the vision on the screen, there lies the ghost of a human mind and body. In Puiu's vision, beyond this ghost, there is the shadow of the other, transcendental author.

Masks Off! *Three Exercises of Interpretation*

Authorship thrives on recognition. By 2012, Romanian directors had become a constant presence in the international film festival circuit. Mungiu's Palme d'Or trophy for *4 Months,* Porumboiu's Un Certain Regard prize for *Police, Adjective,* and Florin Șerban's Golden Bear for

If I Want to Whistle, I Whistle confirmed, to many, the existence of a vigorous *cinema des auteurs* in Romania. Their recognition came in one package with that of another type of author: the actor. Young Romanian actors had also been duly noted by the major festivals: Dorotheea Petre won the Un Certain Regard award for her role in *How I Spent the End of the World,* while Cristina Flutur and Cosmina Stratan won the Cannes Film Festival's Best Actress award for *Beyond the Hills*. Many others (Alexandru Papadopol, Dragoș Bucur, Ioana Flora, Luminița Gheorghiu, Ion Fiscuteanu, or Bogdan Dumitrache) were appreciated at other festivals (in Thessaloniki, Buenos Aires, Los Angeles, Copenhagen, Palm Springs, or Locarno). The rise of the NRC relied on, and promoted, a new type of performance, less histrionic than that of the older, theater-trained Romanian artists. Films were no longer conceived as showcases for a few actors, but as the harmonious expression of an ensemble.

Puiu's contribution in this regard cannot be overlooked, although he was not very familiar with the young graduates of the Romanian films schools. At the National University, the alma mater of most Romanian artists, Mungiu, Porumboiu, Mitulescu, Giurgiu, and Netzer were colleagues and often collaborated with actors such as Alexandru Papadopol, Dragoș Bucur, Ioana Flora, Mimi Brănescu, Bogdan Dumitrache, or Gabriel Spahiu. Puiu did not know them, or, at least, not as well as others in his generation did; yet all the new "faces" he selected through casting sessions would become NRC stars. Papadopol would feature in Mungiu's *Occident* and Spahiu in *Amintiri din Epoca de Aur* (Tales from the Golden Age; 2009). Radu Muntean would rely on Dragoș Bucur for *The Fury* and on Mimi Brănescu for *Tuesday, After Christmas*. Bucur would also be the protagonist of Porumboiu's *Police, Adjective* and Dumitrache would be cast in the same director's *When Evening Falls on Bucharest* and in Netzer's *Child's Pose*.[37] Though not new to cinema, Luminița Gheorghiu has become the iconic figure of the NRC after Puiu cast her in all his films.[38] A few of these actors recognize Puiu's career-changing influence on their art. Of his work for *Stuff and Dough,* Bucur notes,

> I consider I am very much indebted to Puiu for my formation as a film actor. Involuntarily and seamlessly, he taught me a few elementary rules. These belong to every actor's "kitchen" and are difficult to describe. Many times I had heard that thing about people whom you do not meet by chance and

> who influence you for the rest of your life. I did not believe in it. I thought these were stories. (Bucur, "Un rol bun")

Ioana Flora has similar thoughts, "From my experience on *Stuff and Dough* I learned as if from a real school, which was not the case with the university at that time. I am still a Cristi Puiu fan. You cannot but respect the artistic personality of the one who has discovered you, who helped you to express yourself, and who opened you up to acting" ("Interviu"). Puiu eventually ventured into teaching acting and scriptwriting at the university. He is one of the founders of a new approach to the art of acting in Romania, based on direct immersion in a role, that is, on practice rather than standardized, theoretical training.

Direct immersion in a role was the starting point for *Three Exercises*. In 2008, Les Chantiers Nomades, an association that organizes regular workshops for actors, invited Puiu to conduct a session in Grenoble; the result was a series of exercises based on Harold Pinter's *Revue Sketches* (Puiu, "Every Film"). He received the same invitation a few years later and, in the spring of 2011, he went to Toulouse with a new text: the Russian religious philosopher Vladimir Solovyov's *Three Conversations* (Puiu, "Every Film"). The director asked the twelve actors, selected through blind casting, whether they would agree to engage in the actual making of a film rather than in a series of disconnected exercises; they did (Puiu, "Every Film"). Their "scenes" became a film only when, at a friend's insistence, Puiu edited the material for the Rotterdam International Film Festival.

Vladimir Solovyov was not an obvious choice for a "co-scriptwriter." Born in Moscow in 1853, the son of a famous professor, he had, by the age of twenty-seven, obtained his doctorate in philosophy (Ianoşi 5). He soon became one of the prominent Russian philosophers of the time, renowned for the existential overtones of his religious beliefs. His ideas about the world's progress underwent several changes. Solovyov initially believed in the ideal union between Eastern and Western Christianity, with Russia as a mediator; toward the end of his life, however, he wrote about the collapse of this Christian utopia and the arrival of the Antichrist (Ianoşi 7). *Three Conversations* was written in 1900, shortly before his death, at a time when he was profoundly disappointed with the evolution of history.

"Is *evil* only a natural *defect*, an imperfection disappearing by itself with the growth of good, or is it a real *power, ruling* our world by means of temptations, so that to fight it successfully assistance must be found in another sphere of being?" asks Solovyov in the 1900 preface for the work (15). Five characters—the Prince, Mr. Z, a Politician, a General, and a Lady—engage in heated debate around this question. Each represents a distinct viewpoint on the matter. The Prince—whom scholars believe to have been imagined with Leo Tolstoy in mind—argues that, if people were to listen to God, the Good would, eventually, drive away the Evil, which is merely a "defect" (Solovyov 135–36). His opponent, Mr. Z, considers that Evil is a real force in the world, with death as its ultimate incarnation; the only victory over it lies in resurrection (Solovyov 148–49). The General, a traditionalist, does not question his mission to defend his country and religion, and, in the last conversation, does not chime in too often. By contrast, the Politician parades a secular, utopic view that, given peace and the natural progress of culture and civilization, Good would eventually triumph (Solovyov 137). Finally, the Lady, a representative of the upper classes, only functions as a sounding board for their ideas. The characters' discussion turns, relentlessly, to the existence of a different world, beyond death and beyond the senses, a world that can be glimpsed, but to which access is barred by the formulaic dogmas people embrace.

Such an idea is much in tune with Puiu's own philosophy. A self-described rational thinker, he does not express any doubts about the existence of a God, which can be grasped beyond the limits of one's reason and senses. The director is intrigued by the significance of what may appear as simple coincidences, and that, when investigated, may uncover surprising connections among people or may illuminate different moments in one's life. It is an almost mystical faith in a different existential dimension that can be revealed to one only in flashes, on condition that the individual is open to it. All his films chronicle an individual's refusal to see the symbiosis between the profane and the sacred worlds until it is too late, hence the absence of salvation or redemption. Ovidiu thinks himself invincible and dismisses Marcel as inconsequential to his plans, only to understand the depth and reach of the man's malefic influence when it is too late to undo their pact. Similarly, Lazarescu fails to prepare himself for the journey ahead and is blind to the "signs" of a different realm that accompany his trip from hospital to hospital (as is almost everybody else around him). Viorel lives in a self-enclosed universe, isolated from the world of the living by choice and acting upon them as a distant, revengeful, fallen God. The mortals are barred access to the plenitude of the sacred, and to their universal kinship, because they are too much preoccupied with the workings of the profane.

Based on Solovyov's third dialogue, *Three Exercises* continues the director's forays into the relationship between fathers and children, the existence of a transcendental world, and the relationship between cinema and life itself. In Toulouse, the twelve actors were separated into three groups, each with its own dynamics and setting. They were given the same text, but had to improvise around it and make it accessible to contemporary audiences. The first scene features Marion (Bottollier) and Patrick (Vaillant), a married couple of university professors, who have invited their longtime friend and university-fellow Ugo (Broussot) for lunch in their garden. Ugo brings along a childhood acquaintance, Jean-Benoît (Poirier), a French soldier on leave from Afghanistan, with whom the professors have nothing in common. In the second "exercise," Anne-Marie (Charles) and her daughter Ludivine (Anbérrée) also host a lunch for their friends, Diana (Sakalauskaite) and Barnabé (Perrotey), in their small, rather cramped apartment; after a spirited discussion on the nature of the Antichrist, the four sip tea and comment on art cinema. The background for the third sequence is a former armory building converted into artists' studios. Hillary (Keegin), Perrine (Guffroy), Anne (Courpron) and Nathalie (Meunier) have lunch and prepare for the evening. Finally, all characters arrive for the séance, "armed" with lifelong preconceptions. Hillary, an unwilling master of ceremonies, tries to help them engage with each other, but the experiment fails when Ugo breaks into laughter.

One cannot say the same about Puiu's endeavor. Successively embodied by three different individuals, Solovyov's characters acquire distinct personalities within each context and develop particular relationships with the viewer. The exercises seek to demonstrate that, beyond the arguments written on the page, it is the speaker's personality, the manner in which the same ideas are expressed, the emotions projected by each actor or actress, the relationships established among them, and

Figure 16: At lunch

the "participation" of each setting that convey meaning. The chemistry of all these elements constitutes the grounds for spectators' possible epiphanies about life and death.

The weight of the conversation is carried by the opposition between the Prince and Mr. Z on the question of one's relationship with an omnipotent Father (whose existence, however, they do not question, as the Politician does). Both consider that the deterioration of this relationship has led humankind astray. In the Prince's eyes, people live "like mushrooms," for their own pleasure, and this absence of a moral code is the source of permanent conflicts. The cause, he suggests, is the waning faith, respect, and fear for an all-seeing Master. He pleads for a new "catechism" with clear guidelines for ethical behavior. If the Prince dismisses individual freedom as intrinsically pernicious, leading individuals toward a life of instincts, Mr. Z contends that it is the very absence of such freedom that is at the root of conflicts. People get attached to their own versions of truth and justice, and remain blind to the complex, sometimes even contradictory nature of existence. (Viorel, one may notice, is a perfect example of such an individual.) In Mr. Z's vision, only God the Father can deliver this absolute truth, so it is human beings' reluctance to understand their limits that fuels wars. Mr. Z is bothered by the rise of "imposture" as Christians superficially accept and brag about God's existence, but use his name in vain and remain unaware of the reality beyond their own. For both the Prince and Mr. Z, the connection with a central, metaphysical Father is essential to people's relationships with each other: for the one, because it may inculcate fear and self-control, for the other because it opens the human mind to a much richer reality and can inspire empathy with the other. Solovyov's text, therefore, argues in favor of recognizing God not as a distant master, but as a loving parent; God has sacrificed his son to give human beings the opportunity to choose, to be inspired by the good, and to rise to eternal life (Solovyov 148–49, 152–53).

The connection with God as the Father is equally important to Puiu. He describes the Supreme Being as a benevolent figure who respects and nurses the freedom of his mortal "children." In this respect, the Romanian director shares Mr. Z's philosophy (and, implicitly, Solovyov's). It would, however, be inappropriate to describe Puiu's thinking solely as the product of Eastern Orthodoxy. Indeed, he is attracted to the writings of Orthodox monastic figures (such as Arsenie Papacioc or Petre Țuțea), but his spirit is rather eclectic. To him, the historian of art and religion Heinrich Zimmer (whose volume *The King and the Corpse: Tales of the Soul's Conquest of Evil* [1948] he found inspiring), the physicist David Bohm (whose philosophy of the human mind and perception is fascinating to Puiu), and the linguist Alfred Korzybski (whose idea that our epistemological field is necessarily limited by our language and nervous system Puiu also endorses) are equally valid sources of knowledge about human limits and the sacred (Korzybski). The Romanian director was drawn to Solovyov's conversations because they investigated the nature of God rather than question his existence.

None of the three characters giving life to the Prince is endowed with the gravity one might associate with this role. In the first scene, Ugo, a university professor, has nothing in common with his childhood friend, Jean-Benoit, the soldier, yet he invites him to lunch because he hopes to enjoy the "experiment." His Prince is affable and polished, but insincere and snobbish. He adopts an air of innocence and concern, and speaks in favor of a moral code, but is the first to mock others as inferiors when they are not around. By comparison, in the second dialogue, Anne-Marie shies away from debates with her daughter Ludivine because she does not have the stamina to argue with her yet again. She lives surrounded by books and is interested in the occult sciences. Her Prince genuinely believes in God's guidance, but appears powerless and a bit naive. In the third scene, Anne is equally ineffective, though more entertaining. If Ugo sounds cynical and Anne-Marie is unconvincing, Anne appears inexperienced, too gullible, and, when questioned, confused about her own beliefs. A young woman in her thirties, she complains about her lack of success at Internet dating, and seems to have borrowed her ideas about God from someone else, without fully understanding them. Age and gender differ from one character to the next, but what undermines their criticism of people's self-centeredness is their own self-absorption.

Two of the characters impersonating Mr. Z are also self-absorbed, in spite of their judgment of the others' rigid interpretation of the word, be it of God or science. To Ugo's duplicitous Prince, Patrick opposes a condescending Mr. Z, who dismisses his wife Marion's ideas because he perceives her in need of guidance, and disapproves of his friend for his dubious choices and erroneous use of sacred texts. He also looks down on Jean-Benoit because he is of a different class. This arrogant, inflexible Mr. Z does not really fully develop his argument, but merely accuses the others of misinterpreting the Bible. Neither is Ludivine, the second Mr. Z, more persuasive, in spite of her appealing levity of tone and manner. A young student with a tendency to rebel, Ludivine launches into a free interpretation of the Gospels, and rails at the rising imposture of those who use Christ's name to justify their actions. Her Mr. Z is spirited and sharply tongued, but neither persuasive nor emotionally stirring. Hillary will be both. Calm, well-organized, and self-assured, she believes in the possibility of a connection with the world beyond the senses, and convinces others to join her séance.

As in the case of the Prince, it is the characters' relationships with each other that provide an inkling of their deeper nature. Patrick is an expert at reading the Bible, but treats everyone with aloofness, ignoring its calls for meekness and moderation. Ludivine preaches about people's hypocrisy, but is herself too critical of others and blind to her own flaws. Hillary's more easygoing personality and, especially, her ability to move her friends confer on her speech the sincerity that the others are missing. She laments the absence of unconditional love (of people for each other and for God), which almost brings her to tears and prompts her on-screen listeners to reassure her of their support. This moment of the characters' (and, possibly, the actresses') quiet epiphany of their deeper connection with each other is possible only because Hillary reveals her vulnerability, taking off her "mask" of socially expected behavior. It is in hope for such moments of transcendence that Puiu and the actors also engaged in their "exercises."

At the heart of the director's proposal, therefore, lies the relationship between truth and love, and Solovyov's discourse provides the grounds for a philosophical approach to the question. The absence of love (in its absolute sense) is buried—in "civilized" societies especially, as Diana argues—under impenetrable masks, which hide individuals' real intentions, ensure a comfortable living, and may be the conditions for the "culture of peace" (one of the Politician's terms). This disguise demands a constant suppression of the true self, with its desires, necessities, and interests (as Mr. Z suggests), which leads, in the long run, to the return of the repressed, often in violent forms, even directed against the self in the form of neurosis. (In this respect, Solovyov anticipates Sigmund Freud's *Civilization and Its Discontents* [1930]). The more hermetic the masks are, the further people get from an honest communication with each other and the revelation of the sacred and of their oneness through God (as Hillary argues). Indirectly, Puiu's own proposal, in *Three Exercises,* is that love for, and trust in, the other and openness to vulnerability may bring the individual nearer to the experience of the "ineffable," and, through it, to a deeper knowledge and understanding of universal kinship.

Interestingly, his position on the relationship between truth and peace appears somewhat at odds with the one expressed in Solovyov's text. Inspired by Arsenie Papacioc, whose time in the Romanian gulag influenced his vision of (historical) truth, Puiu believes that peace is more important than justice and, therefore, more valuable than establishing truth (which, anyway, is impossible to determine). In his case, however, peace does not result from the polite interaction among people who have learned to hide their thoughts and desires under the mask of civility; peace is the product of a direct and honest engagement with an other undertaken in the spirit of love, kinship, and common interest. It is a rather idealized vision that denies the urgency and weight of one's immediate, physical and historical experience of the world.

Solovyov's, and Puiu's, philosophy relies on the inexpressible experience of a beyond. Puiu credits the imagination with the ability to access the sacred as the only human faculty that can exceed the limits imposed both by sensory perception and rational thinking. In this sense, he echoes Solovyov's belief that true knowledge of the world comes from one's capacity to intuit it, to imagine it following what the Russian philosopher terms as the "ecstatic inspired state" (Gaidenko 123). For the Romanian, the origins of the imagination are also divine, but they imply a persistent awareness of one's boundaries and a constant openness to, and love for, the other.

In *Three Exercises,* the séance provides the opportunity for all characters to achieve such knowledge of the world by means of a "highly intimate" connection with each other, as Hillary defines it. The participants should not be hampered by thoughts about the possible consequences of what they "say or express," but feel free to "act on [themselves]" and come together as a whole. It is, primarily, an occasion for "giving," for being "generous with those present," with their "souls, dreams, and thoughts." The idealistic, impossible nature of such a demand of faith in, and love for, the (largely unknown) other is revealed when, unable to forego their masks, a few of the characters burst into laughter.

Truth, love, and the tearing down of conventional masks are also at the heart of Puiu's theory about acting, which he understands as a search for the self. He defines acting as a mission to inspire, in viewers, an

Figure 17: Communication breakdown |

epiphany of a richer, invisible reality. For such revelation to be possible, the actors need to be fully involved in the moment and forget all other aspects of their public persona. To that effect, he engages his actors in exhaustive rehearsing sessions in search of an "unreflective spontaneity," that is, a spontaneity that is not studied or mimicked, but lived (Ferencz-Flatz 114, 120–21). The direct, complete immersion in the role is the condition for a genuine, convincing performance, the only one that can transcend the screen. Puiu believes that such an endeavor is very difficult because it implies letting go of the fear of being exposed, abandoning all safety nets, and revealing all, including those parts of oneself that are most vulnerable and troublesome. The director's task is, then, to give actors the space to be themselves without losing his own authority—to be a loving Father.

Puiu's relentless search for an actor's close faithfulness to the self sets him apart on the Romanian stage. His approach, however, continues, and adds to, a long tradition of acting that links an actor's inner life to stage performance. In this respect, David Mamet is a kindred spirit in the understanding of acting as an unveiling of the real human being on stage rather than the construction of a particular character (Mamet 39). It is only by "going out there naked" that actors can achieve their purpose: to "move the audience till they [fear] for their soul" (Mamet 7, 30). Truthfulness to one's nature, which Mamet defines as the absence of pretension and manipulation (that is, masks), is the condition for such a powerful effect on the audience. Puiu adds a few mystical notes: acting is an offer of love, as actors surrender themselves, as in a ritual sacrifice, so that viewers "fear for their souls" when faced, for a few, short moments, with the beyond.

Produced as a workshop in acting methods, *Three Exercises* is, ultimately, a commentary on the role that cinema, as art, plays in one's knowledge and understanding of the world around. This unusual film signals its participation in a much larger culture when Diana and Barnabé discuss the works of Šarūnas Bartas, Apichatpong Weerasethakul, and Jafar Panahi. When Diana voices her frustration at the opaqueness of a Thai film, Barnabé responds, "They are people like us," hinting at the broad culture of humanism to which, ideally, all cinema belongs. Like religion or acting, Puiu suggests, cinema is only an occasion for personal epiphanies.

What's in a Name? "Das Spektrum Europas"

The sense that "they are people like us" inspired the very project of the EU. A willing association of nations, the new Europe was to be reborn on ideals of equality, freedom, and solidarity. By 2013, the Union had become a full-blown, supranational organization of twenty-eight states. A "peaceful, united, and prosperous Europe" was to be the stable haven that its inhabitants craved after two horrifying world wars and at least two vicious postcommunist ethnic conflicts ("The History of the European Union").

Nevertheless, the 2008 financial crisis posed various challenges. It exposed the EU Parliament's reduced influence as well as the economic inequality among EU members (Pîrvulescu). The imposed austerity, the virulent protests against it, and the rapid rise of nationalist parties almost everywhere have chipped at the European ideals. The suggestion of a two-tier Europe, in which the seventeen, mostly Western European countries in the Eurozone would have greater power to decide policies, may split the Union into two bodies, one largely comprised of former Eastern European countries that would not be able to participate in all governance matters (Hughes; Hill). By 2015, Euroscepticism and anti-EU parties have proliferated everywhere; the unexpected waves of immigrants have only furthered bolstered their ranks.[39] Today, the project of a united, supranational umbrella for all seems more difficult to achieve than expected (Traynor, "Greece to Face Ultimatum" and "2014: A Rough Year for Europe").

In 2014, the one hundredth commemoration of the Sarajevo attack that ignited World War I drew the attention of many. Several countries organized year-long events that included concerts, exhibitions, conferences, and various other public ceremonies (Quinn, Reverchon, Masci, and Käppner; Henley; Cowell). In Sarajevo, however, a dispute between the Serbian and Bosnian historians gathered at a conference threatened to undermine the event (Hockenos; Associated Press). The smoothed-over European community of spirit and purpose remains fragile, marred by old enmities.

Les Ponts de Sarajevo (Bridges of Sarajevo; 2014) was part of the effort to transform World War I, and Sarajevo in particular, into a European *lieu de memoire*. Conceived by its artistic director Jean-Michel

Frodon as a multivoice reflection on the city's emotional and cultural significance to Europe, the omnibus production includes thirteen films connected to each other by François Schuiten and Luis da Matta Almeida's animated footage. The shorts span almost all cinematic modes and were entrusted to well-established and new-coming directors from across Europe: Bulgaria (Kamen Kalev), Serbia (Vladimir Perisic), Italy (Leonardo di Costanzo and Vincenzo Marra), Germany (Angela Schanelec), Romania (Cristi Puiu), France (Jean-Luc Godard, Ursula Meier, and Islid Le Besco), Ukraine (Sergei Loznitsa), Spain (Marc Recha), Bosnia and Herzegovina (Aida Begic), and Portugal (Teresa Villaverde). The production was equally pan-European: France, Bosnia-Herzegovina, Switzerland, Italy, Germany, Portugal, and Bulgaria share the credits. The problem of the moral, cultural, and even political legacy passed on to future generations is central to fiction films as diverse as Kalev's "My Dear Night," Recha's "Zan's Journey," Villaverde's "Sara and Her Mother," Le Besco's "Little Boy" or Meier's "Quiet Muro." The burden war places on individual conscience animates Di Costanzo's "The Outpost," Schanelec's "Princip, Text," Perisic's "Our Shadows Will," and Marra's "The Bridge." Finally, Godard's "Bridges of Sighs," Loznitsa's "Reflections," and Begic's "Album" are self-reflective about the role of images, architecture, and words in recording and retelling "stories," and, thus, in constantly reorganizing memory and history. Europe, whether during World War I, the Bosnian wars of the 1990s, or today, is home to alliances and betrayals, desertion and resilience, sorrow and promise. Shaped by the centuries-old cohabitation of different cultures, religions, and modes of being, Sarajevo rises not only as the quintessential European city, but also as one of the many hearts of the world.

Thematically, Puiu's "Das Spektrum Europas" stands somewhat apart in the series. The film does mention Gavrilo Princip and the war, but its focus is not on the events themselves. The Romanian's short is a scathing exposure of the enduring legacy of nationalism, xenophobia, and anti-Semitism that has shaped the history of the Balkans, and of Europe itself. Puiu's dark humor makes his analysis slightly more palatable, yet no less caustic in its effects.

On New Year's Eve, Mr. (Marian Râlea) and Mrs. Popescu (Valeria Seciu) prepare to turn in for the night, but not before settling the matter of nations and their "virtues" once and for all. The woman has been reading Hermann Keyserling's *Europe* (*Das Spektrum Europas*), a book first published in 1928, and she wants to share with her husband her delight that Romanians are depicted as "poets" and the descendants of Byzantium. The man, who speaks decisively about a book he has not read, passes on his judgments: the Hungarians, the Americans, and the "Gypsies" are responsible for all the evils in these parts of the world; Keyserling is Jewish and, therefore, biased in his evaluations; and American Jews rule the world. His analysis delivered, he turns over and goes to sleep. The wife stops to meditate for a few seconds, takes off her glasses, and lies down. "It is raining," she whispers, somehow puzzled by the phenomenon as she is puzzled by her husband's acumen and her own cultural ignorance.

What could possibly have attracted Puiu to this obscure book? Keyserling (1880–1946) was a German scholar whose ideas about Europe's evolution and mission were very influential among the aristocracy before World War II. After World War I, a large part of his estate was nationalized by authorities of newly independent Estonia, and Keyserling, married to one of Bismarck's granddaughters, took on an itinerant identity as a public intellectual. He believed his calling was to teach future leaders about the importance of creating a supranational Europe as a counterbalance to both America and Bolshevik Russia. His vision was to be achieved only with the help of a pan-European aristocracy (Gusejnova 122–26). Keyserling himself, however, was a rather curious figure. Dubbed the "red count" by the conservatives and a "conservative aristocrat" by the liberals, he fit neither category very well (Gusejnova 123). His hodge-podge, unflattering depiction of all European nations was based on his early travels across the continent, and he clearly shared the widespread anti-Semitic spirit of the day (Keyserling 345).[40]

Many nations receive their own dose of negative stereotyping. The Englishman is "the animal-man"; the French "emotional rather than intellectual"; and Spain belongs "not to Europe but to Africa," in that its culture is "primeval" (21, 49, 75–76). In most cases, Keyserling has something positive to add: the English are "gifted psychologically"; the French are the most talented Europeans at creating a harmony "between intelligence, soul, body, and the world"; and the Spaniards are "thoroughly and completely unmilitaristic" (27, 45, 79). The Germans, above all, are "an historic phenomenon which only America can parallel," but they remain "misunderstood by everybody" (95). Keyserling's identification with the German nation cannot be more evident.

Such scorching labeling of Europeans has, in the count's view, only one purpose: to make them aware of their own "characteristics" and prepare them to live with each other. "Above all, every nation which looks down upon the others in a delusion of grandeur, believing itself to embody the human ideal, simply makes itself ridiculous," writes Keyserling; he slyly adds that his readers' "sense of humor and superiority" would help them to remember the true spirit of the book as expressed in its motto, "For all of us have sinned and come short of the glory of God" (329, 13). Keyserling seemed to militate for a higher consciousness among Europeans, one built on the mutual appreciation of the good in all nations, and his words sound prophetic of the future EU motto "unity in diversity" (351). If Puiu's film shares anything with the 1928 book it is the belief in the ridiculousness of classifications and epithets. In fact, the Romanian director constantly, and subtly, undermines Keyserling's practices and brings to the fore the absurdity of all labels.

Keyserling's faith is in a Europe superior to all others in culture and spirit (371). Mr. Popescu shares the count's essentialist reasoning, but both remain unaware of their own flaws, an irony not lost on Puiu or his viewers. The Romanian middle-class retiree reads the book's introduction, "All nations are of course thoroughly unpleasant affairs. Man, as such, is a dubious enough sort of creature; only in exceptional cases does a sample of the genus achieve standards which everyone instinctively imposes on everyone else" (Keyserling 7). In the intimacy of his bedroom, away from the "eyes" of public conscience, this man feels free to judge everybody else with little consideration for anything but his own preconceptions. The spirit of the introduction entirely passes him by.

For one, Mr. Popescu lives in a world that, as he obliquely divulges to his wife, is the result of a global conspiracy directed against him. The ones "responsible" for his plight are, as he declares, the "Hungarians, the Americans, and the Gypsies." Romanians have had centuries-long squabbles with the Hungarian minority over the origin and rightful appurtenance of Transylvania, one of the major regions of the country, which was part of the Austro-Hungarian Empire until 1918. The Sarajevo attack, and the world war it engendered, meant, for them, as for many nations in southeastern Europe, the completion of a long-desired unification. If the Hungarians are threatening because of their potential territorial claims, the "Gypsies," that is, the Roma community, are stereotyped as possibly criminal. Former slaves, gradually liberated in the eighteenth and nineteenth century, the Roma continue to be one of the most marginalized minorities in Europe.

Why the Americans? Mr. Popescu will "explain" a bit later: because "absolutely every major event in the history of this wretched planet was planned by these American Jews" (not that he is not an equal opportunity offender: he fully admits he dislikes Arabs as well). At the core of his conspiracy theories is his identification with the position of the victim. His "enemy" is so omnipotent and omnipresent that it haunts the entire post-1989 history of Romania. "Everything else has gone down the drain," Mr. Popescu tells his wife; "Industry, gymnastics, agriculture, the whole lot," he adds. A member of the precariat classes, like Tomescu and Lazarescu, he decries the fall of a great nation (after all, he is the product of communism, when everything was grand and glorious) and can find no other explanation but the occult forces that have banded against his kin.

Interestingly, he is somewhat at odds with dominant public opinion in Romania. Most of the population was satisfied when the country joined the EU in January 2007. On average, Romanians knew little about the EU, but believed in it for the same reason they believed in the Church: because it gave them hope (Lungu). In spite of a short-lived slump in optimism after the 2008 financial crisis, people seem happy with the personal advantages (freedom of movement, increased security, and improved social protection) they have enjoyed since 2007 (Brown, Murray et al.; Neagu; "După şase ani"). They do, however, believe that the state has been gradually subordinated to the invisible decision makers in Brussels ("MAI 2015"). The divorce between the individual and the nation-state in the consciousness of many is also a reflection of their general mistrust of local authorities. Many Romanians love Europe because they are not too enamored with how their own institutions work.

Mr. Popescu is a Eurosceptic. He lived, for many years, in an isolated, xenophobic, and nationalist totalitarian regime, and old habits rarely go away. He is also too old to take advantage of the economic and cultural mobility promised by the EU. To him, everything is falling apart because he senses that his own life is slipping away and nothing can be more glamorous, and more distant, than his own youth. The implied nostalgia and fear of the future somewhat temper what many viewers may regard as his offensive comments.

The same character is a maestro at undermining the history told by others, but remains blind, willfully so, to his own "methods" (a characteristic he has in common with Keyserling). In this respect, "Das Spektrum Europas" shares, with other films in the *Bridges of Sarajevo* project, an interest in the ways in which books construct knowledge and memory. His strategy is not without its virtues: he questions the time period, the author, and the purpose of the book with no other immediate gain but to teach his wife a lesson. Not only is the book written after World War I, and so the writer is not a gifted clairvoyant, as Mrs. Popescu seems to imply, but its author is Jewish, says Popescu. The purpose of the entire undertaking is, therefore, less to clarify than to confuse innocent "victims" like his wife. There is no other clue for such a conclusion but the author's name, but it is enough for the man. Ironically, Keyserling, who was not Jewish, was just as anti-Semitic as Mr. Popescu, and both advertise their biased convictions under the mask of objectivity.

Commenting on the significance of Keyserling's name, Mr. Popescu ends his cogitations, "Don't you know what they say? Ionescu, formerly Rabinovitch." His "what's in a name" moment is, from a much different perspective, Puiu's own. "Das Spektrum Europas" scrutinizes the ways in which people easily attach labels and isolate themselves from those around them. For Mr. Popescu, Europe and its peoples are reduced to what he can imagine about them from inside his bedroom in Bucharest.

The city is a central metaphor to the film's discourse. In the opening scene, the popular song "Bucharest, Bucharest" can be heard coming, probably, from the Popescus' neighbors. Sung by Gică Petrescu, very famous in Romania for his New Year's Eve party songs, this paean to the city is seeped with nostalgia for a long-gone world. In his rationale for the film, Puiu writes, "I can see that the city is, more and more, the cold wall of the fortress that protects us against all those who are our neighbors. . . . The city is the failed project of the meeting with the Other" ("Motivație regizorală"). The city, as a metonymy for the nation and even for supranational entities like the EU, is a prison, confining and dangerously enmeshed in its own worldview. Through Mr. Popescu, the Romanian filmmaker draws attention to the generalized closing in of walls within the "city" itself, where, in spite of instantly available information, people live isolated within their own comfortable imaginary cells. All opinions repressed in the public sphere by the EU discourse of brotherly unity are left to roam free within the intimate sphere of the couple (and of the bedroom). It is a situation eerily reminiscent of the roots for the outbreak of World War I.

Two other narrative devices also contribute to the director's investigation: character construction and irony. In spite of their narrow outlook upon their neighbors, the spouses are sketched with a loving eye for their idiosyncrasies. Mrs. Popescu is subdued and turns to her life partner with a schoolgirl's confidence and deference. She is a naive reader who takes everything at face value, including her husband's preposterous comments. Mr. Popescu may look condescendingly at his wife for her "blunders" and "misunderstandings," and he is silenced by her apparent inability to follow his "profound" comments, but he never puts her down. There is a rather moving choreography of their gestures and dialogue: when she is putting on her glasses, he is taking his off and vice versa; when she reads from the book, he patiently waits for her to finish, and she does the same when he browses through the pages. The cohesion and peace among them are the effects of time and the mutual acceptance of their power positions within the marriage; they are also the products of the couple's obliviousness to their own deficiencies. The Popescus belong to the educated middle classes, but they are stuck in an old, patriarchal universe out of tune with the times. The woman is puzzled by what a "spectral analysis" may mean, but, when her husband compares it to an MRI, both fail to understand the mediated, incomplete relationship between representation and reality. To them, as to Keyserling, their own limited vision of the world is the only one.

If the harmony between the spouses stimulates viewers' empathy for their weaknesses, the film also engages their analytical faculties by means of irony and humor. Mr. Popescu's gross overstatements, his wife's unlimited approval and admiration, and the setting for their discussion play a major role in this sense. Their combination was inspired by an old Romanian play, *Mr. Leonida Faces the Reactionaries* (Conu' Leonida față cu reacțiunea), written by Ion Luca Caragiale in 1880. Caragiale is the national playwright, renowned for his acid humor and corrosive criticism of social and political mores in nineteenth-century Romania. His

Figure 18: Bedroom harmony

sense of the absurd (of language and situations) is undeniably part of the NRC's cultural legacy. *Mr. Leonida* is a one-act play in which an elderly couple prepare to go to bed and discuss the possibility of a revolution. The husband straightforwardly denies it, given that the government does not allow guns in the city. The two are scared stiff by some explosions they hear, thinking that shots have been fired, only to be "saved" by their maid, who comes in the morning and reassures them that what they heard was merely the celebration of the beginning of Lent.

Mr. and Mrs. Popescu share their prototypes' fear of the world outside their windows. Like Caragiale's characters, Puiu's make comical remarks and have no sense of proportion, cultural or otherwise (Mr. Popescu recommends to his wife an internationally obscure novel by Vintilă Corbul, as if it held the absolute, and secret, truth about the world. He also suggests that, because Corbul's son worked for the same company he did, he himself had been touched by the father/writer's glory). Such irony is not diminished by the tender drawing of controversial characters, but only contributes to the complex portrait Puiu paints of them. The filmmaker indirectly comments on the constancy of human nature, on its conservative tendencies and its rush toward facile, immediate "explanations" for otherwise complex phenomena.

The choice of *mise en scène* equally demands an inquisitive eye as nostalgia is tempered by warnings about its effects. A reproduction of Nicolas Poussin's *Et in Arcadia Ego* (1637–1638) looms over the couple, as a reminder of the paradise human beings may lose once they gain awareness of their own mortality (Steefel Jr. 100–101; Thompson 20). It also suggests regret for a dying, simpler world, with its promise of security and stability. The shape of the bed's headboard, which mimics that of old tombstones, reinforces the same sense of human transience, as does the chosen time for the sketch (New Year's Eve, a time of passing). The film's epiphany is, again, that of the imperfect nature of the profane world and its blindness to the presence of the sacred. The surplus of wistfulness is somewhat diluted by a seemingly inconsequential prop: the baby highchair at the living-room table. This small detail raises questions about what exactly and how much of their grandparents' legacy the new generation will remember and impart to their offspring (a preoccupation shared by Puiu's other films).

The disjunction between the couple's limited perception and the world out there, between the individual's fragmented knowledge and the wholeness of life, is further reinforced in the intermittent flashing of the Christmas tree lights, as mere reminders of the darkness that surrounds them. In the same sense, the dogs heard howling from time to time and the rain coming down in the end function as unseen messengers of the streets and time beyond this small apartment. The camera's fixed point of view, as well as the framing of the scene within the space permitted by the bedroom doorway, both staples of Puiu's cinema, equally reflect on the film's restricted ability to depict characters and their beliefs, underscoring the fictional nature of any such undertaking. The "spectral analysis of Europe," a term as appropriate for Puiu's film as for the entire *Bridges of Sarajevo* project, turns into the "spectral analysis" of the very art of cinematic representation.

Bridges of Sarajevo was released on May 22, 2014 at the Cannes Film Festival. Later that year it traveled to Sarajevo and Pesaro, where it was screened as part of the centennial celebration and a film festival, respectively. It returned to the Sarajevo Film Festival in August 2014, and it was then released in cinemas in Bosnia and Herzegovina ("World Premiere of 'Bridges of Sarajevo'"; "The Bridges of Sarajevo"). The film addressed the very specific, exclusive audience of art film cinema and has remained unavailable on DVD. *Bridges of Sarajevo* is an ephemeral fragment of memory and history constructed with a tender, yet critical eye to human weaknesses.

Father Is Gone: *Sieranevada*

The third in the Bucharest series, *Sieranevada* is Puiu's most complex project to date. Produced by Mandragora, with funds from the NCC and the EU, the film is still in production at the moment this essay is being written.[41] This new text examines the complicated legacies fathers bequeath their sons and daughters, with a keen eye for what is left unsaid and unchallenged. The passing of the father is commemorated, forty days later, as is tradition, by his family and friends, but some commotion ensues with the arrival of unexpected guests. Within the span of a few hours, in the widow's crammed apartment, the mourners discuss everything from the 9/11 attacks to the virtues and evils of communism, and the role of religion for the twenty-first century generation. Eventually, they do some remembering.

At the core of this new film is Puiu's current preoccupation with a desacralized world, populated by people blind to what he calls the "cosmic dimension" of their existence, even at the most sensitive moments in their lives (Puiu, "Interviu"). In Orthodoxy, the soul of the dead still wanders among the living for forty days, seeking solace. Ironically, the family gathered to mark the final passing of the father barely remembers him, even when, as Puiu suggests, he is watching them from beyond the grave (the camera is intended as a stand-in for the departed; never acknowledged, it follows everybody with love) (Puiu, "Interviu"). The director suggests that, if *Mr. Lazarescu* focused on the experience of the victim (or the actor) and *Aurora* on that of the author (the director), *Sieranevada* tells the story of those who are left behind (the viewers) (Puiu, "Interviu").

Several other signature themes reappear: the strained relationship between generations; the social tensions generated by the workings of capitalism; and nostalgia for one's youth. The context, however, has changed. These are the times of a new, shrinking world, in which contradictory information is readily available at the click of a mouse, big corporations have replaced the mom and pop stores of earlier times, fairy tales have become a matter of performance, and the man next door is fighting in overseas wars. It is also a world of withdrawal: into the past, into religion, and, more importantly, into the increasingly fragmented space of the family. The city has expanded into other, computer-generated continents, and its dwellers may meet face to face, but keep their distance from each other for most of the real-time duration of the plot. The film, therefore, reaffirms Puiu's interest in the conditions that foster or inhibit genuine human connection, in Bucharest or elsewhere.

Sieranevada also examines a world devoid of the physical presence of the father, in which women share the stage with men. It is not the first time they do so: Caty, Ovidiu's mother, Mioara, the paramedic, or Gina, Pușa, and Rodica, and even Mrs. Popescu are important figures in the lives of the different protagonists. They are not the center of the filmmaker's investigation, however, and, to some degree, this is expected of a man who insists on faithfulness to one's own experience: Puiu focuses on male characters because women's experiences are, necessarily, more foreign to his consciousness. In his films, women possess a certain power over the men in their care, even if, sociopolitically, they are equally unable to change their fate (Caty, Mioara, and Gina are cases in point). They also claim their rights, use their charms when necessary, and impose their will when they need to (Betty, Mioara's nurse friend, and even Viorel's ex-wife are good examples). Even if they are more intuitive, women remain as much in the dark about the world they inhabit as men do (so do Caty, Pușa, and Mrs. Popescu).

Puiu's female characters, however, are not much different from others in the NRC who, as Pop suggests, are often portrayed as "unholy mothers," incapable of "giving meaning" to their children, that is, of aiding in their initiation into the sacred (Pop 151–52). One may argue that, at the origin of such a portrayal, there is widespread apprehension of the increasingly visible role women play, socially and politically, in the postcommunist, globalized world.

In *Sieranevada*, women dominate men: they order them around, have better insights into their lives, and even viciously attack them (not without provocation or reason, however). The one exception among so many castrating figures is, possibly, the most empathetic, benign character in the NRC: a pregnant woman (a Virgin Mary figure), she is attuned to the pain of others and inclined to make peace among the different fighting couples. These women are more interesting characters than the men, who seem to enter a new era. The departure of the father has brought about a new order, whose flaws and merits are yet to be explored.

At the end of his rationale for *Sieranevada*, Puiu writes, "If cinema is an anthropological instrument, and if fiction film extracts its material predominantly from within the author's mind in order to become a confession, then, for this confession to be complete, the author's presence and that of the cinematographic apparatus must themselves be revealed/denounced" (Puiu, "*Sieranevada*: intenție regizorală" 3). The Romanian director has constantly increased his attention to the medium and its limitations. Cinema is only a means to underscore the ever-spreading blindness to the sacred of a profane world that thinks itself all-seeing.

Notes

1. All quotes or references to Cristi Puiu's opinions in this essay are based on the interview included in this volume unless otherwise indicated.

2. For example, Ginette Vincendeau's brief description of the most important European filmmakers does not mention any Romanian director (444–45).

3. Ilinca Călugăreanu's *Chuck Norris vs. Communism* (2015) documents the rise of clandestine spectatorship of American films circulating on VHS tapes in the 1980s Romania.

4. The December 1989 events fulfill this criterion, as director Andrei Ujică has indicated (Gorzo, *Lucruri* 230).

5. Puiu's act of stripping himself naked as Viorel in *Aurora* is the visual equivalent of his many other press declarations; it is rather ironical that some have seen this shower scene as unnecessary.

6. Cristian Tudor Popescu argues that this relaxation was, in fact, obtained by a group of directors who asked the Party representatives for "help" in improving the quality of Romanian cinema (235–38).

7. In the case of other visual and plastic arts, there is a turn toward neoexpressionism and neofiguratism, both perceived in opposition to the official, "realist" art (Cârneci 158–62).

8. Václav Havel has argued that the citizens of the former Eastern bloc adopted two attitudes toward the communist regimes: some "lived within a lie,"

accepting and behaving in accordance to authorities' expectations, while others sought to "live within the truth," opposing official discourse (31, 39).

9. In some cases, moral and financial reparations came only after Romania was forced by the European Court of Human Rights court to do so ("La CEDH condamne la Roumanie").

10. Marshal Ion Antonescu was the de facto ruler of Romania during its alliance with Hitler and the Romanian Holocaust. He is the protagonist of Sergiu Nicolaescu's *Oglinda* (The Mirror; 1993) and *The Death Triangle*. The most productive director of the communist era, Nicolaescu was among the most vocal in opposing the NRC. Daneliuc's *A unsprezecea poruncă* (The Eleventh Commandment; 1991) and Nicolae Mărgineanu's *Undeva în est* (Somewhere in the East; 1991) focus on the 1940s and 1950s, respectively.

11. Pintilie's *Balanța* (The Oak; 1992) and *Prea târziu* (Too Late; 1997), Daneliuc's *Patul conjugal* (The Conjugal Bed; 1993) and *Senatorul melcilor* (The Snails' Senator; 1995), and Gulea's *Vulpe—vânator* (Fox: Hunter; 1993) and *Stare de fapt* (State of Things; 1995) are exemplary in this respect.

12. Juan Antonio Bardem described the Spanish cinema of the 1950s as one "of painted dolls," "politically ineffective," "socially false," "intellectually worthless," "aesthetically nonexistent," and "industrially crippled." 1980s Romanian cinema displayed the same "qualities," many of which crossed over into the 1990s (22).

13. *The Retirement Home* employs what Bill Nichols terms as the "participatory mode" of documentary filmmaking, in which the presence of the camera and the crew are revealed to the viewer, as is their direct interaction with the "subjects" (115–16).

14. Rădulescu would also write scripts for many other directors, including Radu Muntean and Călin Peter Netzer.

15. In Cristian Nemescu's *California Dreamin'* (2007), Bobby Păunescu's *Francesca* (2009), or Cristian Mungiu's *Dincolo de dealuri* (Beyond the Hills; 2012), protagonists think that their "salvation" is immediately within their reach if they immigrate. The main characters in Corneliu Porumboiu's *Visul lui Liviu* (Liviu's Dream; 2004) and *Polițist, adjective* (Police, Adjective; 2009), Florin Șerban's *Eu când vreau să fluier, fluier* (If I Want to Whistle, I Whistle; 2010), and Bogdan George Apetri's *Periferic* (Outbound; 2010) get increasingly angry at a system that leaves them little room to make choices.

16. All translations from Romanian into English will be my own unless otherwise noted.

17. The other significant awards had been the 1957 Palme d'Or for Best Short Film for Ion Popescu-Gopo's animated *O scurtă istorie* (A Short History) and the 1965 Best Director Award at the Cannes Film Festival for Liviu Ciulei for *Pădurea spânzuraților* (Forest of the Hanged).

18. The same year (2004), Gus Van Sant's *Elephant* (2003) received the Palme d'Or award and Peter Jackson won the Oscars for *Lord of the Rings: The Return of the King* (2003).

19. Similar cases would occur in 2009, 2012, and 2014. In all, the eerie resemblance with Puiu's film was mentioned by the media ("Crestem spaga"; Mototolea; Marinov).

20. By 2006, more than two million Romanians had resettled, especially in Spain, Italy, Canada, and the United States (Boia, *România* 196).

21. The conceptualization of the camera-observer's presence in anthropological research has its roots in the 1970s, when the term "observational cinema" designated a new approach to research that precluded interpretation of disparate recordings in favor of direct, real-time observation (Grimshaw and Ravetz 3–10).

22. Weak or absent fathers, who belong to all social categories, appear in NRC films from Cătălin Mitulescu's *Cum mi-am petrecut sfârșitul lumii* (How I Spent the End of the World; 2006) to Mungiu's *4 Months*, Radu Jude's *Cea mai fericită fată din lume* (The Happiest Girl in the World; 2009), Muntean's *Marți, după Crăciun* (Tuesday, After Christmas; 2010), and Călin Peter Netzer's *Poziția copilului* (Child's Pose; 2013).

23. In a study done by the World Bank in 2000, more than 60 percent of patients reported having paid some form of bribery to a doctor, and around 30 percent declared that they did so at the request of the doctor. The doctors' low salaries were blamed for this situation, as most patients were trying to ensure prompt and proper care in exchange for the bribe ("Diagnostic Surveys of Corruption in Romania").

24. Dr. Mirică will be the protagonist of *Sieranevada* (2016).

25. A young doctor in the first year of practice could have received less than $20 per month, which was even less than in 1991 (Perețianu).

26. Puiu would "recycle" the character of Gina Filip as Viorel's lover in *Aurora*. In the 2010 film, Gina is divorced, but her ex-husband is not Dragoș Popescu. Instead of supplying more information, *Aurora* only complicates the woman's life "story."

27. He will also be taken to surgery by another, invisible "Virgil" (a nurse in the last hospital), and Dr. Anghel ("angel" in Romanian) will operate on him.

28. The Filmmakers' Union did not award the Grand Prize in 2005 at all; it would do the same in 2007 (when Cristian Mungiu's *4 Months* won the Palme d'Or, the first in the history of Romanian cinema).

29. TIFF was established in 2002 by director Tudor Giurgiu and film critic Mihail Chirilov.

30. For example, Mungiu's *4 Months* grossed about $1.2 million in Romania (where it was seen by roughly 90,000 viewers, the highest number of all the NRC productions) and about $8.6 million abroad (Radu, 151; "4 Months, 3 Weeks, 2 Days").

31. In 2006, under the pressure of civil society, and to solidify Romania's bid for the EU, the state officially condemned communism. The victims of communism, however, have yet to be compensated for their suffering, while many former Securitate officers continue to enjoy good pensions (Day).

32. Her earlier comment in Romanian is even more suggestive: "Da' cu tine ce-i, așa, cu noaptea-n cap?" (an approximate translation would be, "Why have you come here so early in the morning, the night still on your mind?"). Puiu marks not only the moment—the dawn (or "aurora" in Romanian)—but also the man's blurry thoughts and his association with the forces of darkness. A close analysis of Puiu's scripts would reveal his exquisite flair for language.

33. An in-depth analysis of the castrating feminine figures in Puiu's films may yield intriguing results.

34. The word may have several meanings: "father" (in English, if we disregard the accent); "dead" (in Swedish); or "deed" (in Danish and Norwegian). In our conversations, Puiu has denied having "produced" this graffiti.

35. In Romanian, the word "stylo" (pen) translates as "stilou." Viorel uses the word "pix" (meaning "ball-pen"), but, given the rarity of people who still use a pen, one may interpret it as a reference to the *auteur* debate.

36. Sobchack argues that each film both perceives ("views") the world and expresses it; in its turn, a viewer can "see" not only what the film "sees," but also that (and how) the film "sees" (56).

37. *Child's Pose* won the Golden Bear Award in 2013.

38. Gheorghiu may be familiar to international audiences because of her roles in Michael Haneke's *Code inconnu* (Code Unknown; 2000) and *Le Temps du loup* (Time of the Wolf; 2003). After *Mr. Lazarescu*, she would star in *12:08 East of Bucharest*, *4 Months*, *Beyond the Hills*, *Child's Pose*, and *Aferim!* (2015).

39. The U.K. Independence Party and the Italian Movimento Cinque Stelle, profoundly Eurosceptic yet belonging to opposite political traditions, are part of the Europe of Freedom and Direct Democracy (EFDD) group ("Results of the 2013 European Elections").

40. Ironically, the book was translated into English by Maurice Samuel, a Jewish philosopher of Romanian origin.

41. This brief discussion of *Sieranevada* is based upon a pre-release screening of the unfinished film. I thank the director for his generous invitation.

Interview with Cristi Puiu

Interview conducted July 4, 2014, and July 27, 2015

MONICA FILIMON: How did you get interested in cinema?

CRISTI PUIU: I got interested in it by chance. I changed direction when I was in Geneva and I left painting for film. I started studying cinema out of curiosity and in complete innocence, fully aware of my lack of knowledge. To make up for it, at one point I used to watch six films a day at home, on VHS tapes. I needed to understand what was going on in cinema because the idea intrigued me.

I also had a few professors and fellow students who helped me. Cédric, my classmate, gave me *A Woman under the Influence* (1974); I watched it and thought, "What foolishness. . . ." I had studied painting and Kurosawa was a god for me. "It's badly shot . . ." I couldn't find my place. "What is it with this film?" The next day I watched it again and I got interested in it. I watched it again that evening and that was it: that was the director for me. I went and got all Cassavetes's films in order to understand them. At the same time, one of my professors was Jean-André Fieschi, who was part of the Jean Eustache group. I only watched *La Maman et la putain* (The Mother and the Whore; 1973) in 2000, when I visited my aunt in England during the summer break. That's how things happened. I used to come back for the summer while I was a student, and took my video player and television set to Răzvan [Rădulescu] to watch films. I was trying to share a certain type of cinema with others, but, at the time, I never had any idea of what Romanian cinema could become.

As a result, when I returned to Romania, I was able to make films without any kind of mental obstacles, without the "corset" that Romanian directors "inherit" from the Bucharest film school. I had nothing like that; I was completely free. I always approach each of my films as the last thing I will do on earth, so I have nothing to lose and can follow my ideas to the end. [. . .]

MF: Have the various changes in Romanian legislation affected your work?

CP: I am probably the last person to talk about the law. Like everybody else, I can identify its flaws, but I don't think I can offer a solution. My only solution cannot work because it is based on trust and that does not work in Romania. I hope we will all be able one day, as the technology advances, to make films with the amount of money we buy bread. After the 2003 scandal, I was so depressed that I went home and decided to start my own company and had one concept in mind: "films made with the money for bread" or "films made on the fly."[1] I started writing and came up with the synopses for the *Six Tales from the Outskirts of Bucharest*. Then I called Răzvan [Rădulescu] and we began to develop them; the first in the series was *Mr. Lazarescu*. I was very desperate at the time and thought that I would make them on VHS and in a very rough way. Suddenly, when I won the Golden Bear, I thought that things might work out and that my quality as a director would not be questioned anymore. But that was not the case. There were further scandals, before and after *Mr. Lazarescu*.

MF: Did *Mr. Lazarescu* recover the initial investment?

CP: No. The films that cannot recuperate their investment will become the property of NCC because this is the contract. That is all that can be said about the relationship between my films and money.

MF: *Aurora* was made with funds from France, Germany, and Switzerland. Does the relationship with European partners count more than the one with Romanian sponsors?

CP: It counts a lot, but I don't know if it counts more because—and here I am telling you about my own experience—when I was looking for financing for *Mr. Lazarescu,* I was told that, if I wanted European money for the film, I first had to receive money from Romanian agencies, and then everybody else would agree to coproduce the film. I don't know how much truth there is in this; that's another discussion. I've only made three feature films so far and the NCC was financially involved in all three.[2]

MF: Is there a "new cinema" because a few directors wanted to make films and did everything they could to do it?

CP: Yes. The same applies to other economic sectors; if they function well in Romania, it is because a few people made them work.

MF: Should the Romanian state do more?

CP: What is needed is a feasible policy for cinema. But nobody is interested in it. Why should they be? During Ceaușescu's times, things were more bluntly assumed: propaganda justified everything. Things have got complicated a lot now because, in reality, no political party has had, in the past twenty years, a clear ideology, in spite of their words. In fact, all they did was to take over the production means and resources. This was the result of the absence of an ideology, and, although I am disgusted by the very word "ideology," such an ideology would imply a certain vision, a perspective on things, a strategy, etc. To a major ideology one could associate a secondary one—a philosophy, a cultural policy—that could make cinema possible in Romania, regardless of the type of cinema one envisions. But such a discourse does not exist. Everything is played by ear, and what is now replacing a coherent cultural policy for cinema is a very dangerous thing: the prize. The prize—in Cannes, Berlin, anywhere—is the first criterion and it's not ok. It's not ok because films cannot always be quantified. In many cases, the films that win prizes are films made for the present moment; the more we advance and the faster technology progresses, the more important the present moment becomes. People are attuned to the present and appreciate a certain film in the present, but, two-three years later, the same film becomes obsolete. Then there are films that keep coming back. [. . .]

MF: The first film you made, together with Andreea Păduraru, after your return was a documentary titled *The Retirement Home*. How did the project start?

CP: Andreea had just got a grant to make a documentary, and she asked me if I wanted to participate in the project. I was ready to collaborate with her. We wanted to see if we could work within an observational documentary convention. We were not able to do it, but we did gather a lot of material that, even if it was not observational in nature, had a certain coherence. It became important to have a voiceover that would explain the one-week experience at that institution. It was important for us to say what that was.

MF: One of the most touching moments is the last one, when the camera silently watches one of the nurses washing an old, paraplegic man. How did you manage to film it?

CP: Here's how. Marius Panduru, the cinematographer, and Andreea Păduraru are from Craiova. After filming at that hospital, we spent about a week, thinking, and we realized it was absolutely necessary to film the moment when a nurse washes up one of the old men. "No, it is indecent," said Marius. I told him, "No, it is not. It is indecent for you because you do not want to look because you are afraid of death. I am also afraid of death. But I find it absolutely obligatory to have this moment—that is where old age and bodily decay take each of us. If not, what exactly are you doing? You silence exactly this type of experience out of modesty." And I also told him, "It does not matter what you film; what matters is how you film it."

We, then, talked with one of the officials, and he made sure, as in the "good old days," to arrange everything for us: a clean, well-made bed and a certain old man, specifically chosen, were waiting for us. The old man had not soiled himself, but the nurse was supposed to "wash" him for the camera.

We got there and we filmed it. Because we were working on some BETA tapes that had already been used, we went to a local television station to check if our own recording had no flaws. When we got there, I realized that Marius had not filmed the moment. I mean, he recorded some images, but they could not be used for our documentary. "Why did you do this?" I asked him. "I could not do it; it was pornography," he replied. "It's not up to you to decide whether it is pornography or not," I responded.

In a way, the good thing about Marius's decision not to film was that everything happened on a Friday or Saturday. By the time we watched the tapes and discussed everything, all the administrative personnel had left the institution. When we went back, people let us in because they had already got used to us and knew we had permission to film. We got in and went looking for a patient. And then we saw Mr. Popescu and the nurse who was getting ready to wash him. We asked her if we could get in and film, and she said, "Yes, son, you can." Then we asked Mr. Popescu if we could film the moment. "Yes, film it," he said. Without his permission, we would not have done it. It was difficult to watch. That entire documentary is about this one moment at the end.

MF: What did you tell your "subjects" about the reason why you were filming them?

CP: We told them it was a workshop project. We had problems with that because they were upset that they would not be seen on national television. We could not satisfy their wish, though.

MF: What was the fate of this documentary? Where was it screened?

CP: I think it was screened in schools. It was the product of a workshop, so it could not be distributed. I am, however, very attached to that experience, which was a trigger for *Mr. Lazarescu*.

MF: Two years later, in 2000, you were involved in a new project, *Archive of Pain*, an installation made in collaboration with Ștefan Constantinescu. Was it an attempt at recovering part of the memory of the communist gulag?

CP: Yes, it was. I have known Ștefan Constantinescu since 1987, I think. When Emil Constantinescu won the elections in 1996, Ștefan saw an opportunity to set up a Web site where former torturers could log in and write about the evil that they had done to others.[3] I thought it would not work because nobody would willingly declare that he or she had once tortured people. What we could do, however, was to record the testimonials of the people who had been through the communist prisons.

We met about twenty people and recorded their stories. I think each interview lasted, on average, about four hours. They were old people.

. . . Out of the twenty interviews, we selected twelve and edited them. We decided to build an installation and project the interviews. Now I regret it because I think it would have been better if the interviews had been only audio and not video. Thanks to the late Mihai Oroveanu, we were able to exhibit this installation in Bucharest; then it travelled to Vilnius and Stockholm. In 2014, there was renewed interest in it, but, unfortunately, all interviews had been recorded on VHS tapes and they were damaged. Now I have to restore them . . .

MF: A second recuperation of memory.

CP: Yes; in a way, yes.

MF: Why was 2001 a good year for Romanian cinema?

CP: 2001 was not a good year for Romanian cinema. 2001 seems to be, in retrospect, the year of a beginning with *Stuff and Dough*. The reaction to totalitarianism, to the war, to the horrors of a dictatorship, which was immediate in Italy, for example, and manifested itself in Italian neorealism, is probably connected to the inner rhythms, very specific and very mysterious, of each nation. We Romanians move in slow motion, so there needed to be a confusing period between 1989 and 2001 before anything important could happen.

MF: Today, *Stuff and Dough* stands out from other films made at the time because of its "unpolished" aesthetics and, especially, the limited perspective of the plot and the characters. What role does the camera play in the film?

CP: The camera adopts the operator's position. I told Silviu [Stavilă], the cinematographer, "We're not going to put the camera on the hood of the van. The camera is the fourth character, so it can only go where the operator can go with it." The storyteller is in the story, and the storyteller is a human being, not a device, not a recording camera. There is a human being there who is watching and choosing parts of the story. That human being is present there, like the invisible man. This is not an invention; it is all about the rigor of using some of the methods of the observational documentary.

In both *Stuff and Dough* and *Mr. Lazarescu*, the camera follows the inner impulses of the one who is filming; that was essential to me. My strategies belong to the tradition of direct cinema, which is not my invention. I returned to Romania with the desire to make my films, and without any intention to start a "revolution" [. . .]. I wanted to make this film; only 60 percent of what I had in mind materialized in it, but this was the direction I wanted and felt I needed to follow.

MF: *Cigarettes and Coffee*, your next film, exposes the tense relationship between a father and a son. The most insignificant details take on profound connotations. For example, the father mentions that his employer is UCECHIM. Is it UCECHIM or ICECHIM?

CP: I may have chosen UCECHIM so that it was a bit different from ICECHIM.[4] I grew up in Ozana, Elena Ceaușescu's "dominion." I attended the Chemistry High School and we all had "internships" at the pharmaceutical company, the paint production factory, the soap production factory, and other similar companies in the area. That's the origin of the word. One cannot invent details like this one. Actually, the entire narrative line is a wink at Ceaușescu's "Golden Age."

MF: It is also a wink at other films.

CP: Yes. It is a wink at Jim Jarmusch, of course. I could not have called the restaurant anything else but Graceland. The coffee and apple pie . . . That is why the short is dedicated to Bella Molnar, the protagonist in *Stranger than Paradise* (1984). That film was a trigger. I seriously thought about making films after watching Jarmusch's *Stranger than Paradise*.

But Jarmusch is not the only reference. When I did the casting, I initially selected Ionel Mihăilescu to play the son. He had played the son in Stere Gulea's *The Moromete Family*, in which Victor Rebengiuc, the father in *Cigarettes and Coffee*, had also played the father. But Mihăilescu did not work, so I had to replace him with Mimi Brănescu.

I did play with such references. They are more than simple references to other films, however; they are an author's "signature." The author deliberately admits that the film is a film; not necessarily a game, but not far from it. The really important "things" are somewhere else, within the object itself, in the way this "object" is connected to others beyond it. Truth lies somewhere beyond all this, in the little and very little details.

MF: Were such "connections" at the origins of *Mr. Lazarescu*?

CP: Yes. That final scene in *The Retirement Home* was one source. I rewatched it several times when I worked on *Mr. Lazarescu*. I showed Oleg Mutu [the cinematographer] and Ioan Fiscuteanu (Mr. Lazarescu) how the nurse washed the old man. Fiscuteanu's wife, who played one of the nurses in *Mr. Lazarescu*, mimics the gestures of that nurse. I could not have invented that. Anyway, *The Retirement Home* was, in a sense, at the roots of this film.

So were my personal experiences in hospitals. When I had an appendectomy in 1997, Anca took me to the emergency room at the Floreasca Hospital.[5] I had no idea who the surgeon was. After he checked my abdomen and told me I was going to have surgery, I kept asking the caretakers around, "Is he a good doctor?" All the hallways were full of patients. They no longer had enough space in the regular wards and everybody was in the hallway. And that's where they "parked" me, too: on a couch in the waiting room. At one point, they moved me in between two beds, on another couch. Before me, an old man had hernia surgery, and, when they brought him back, they put him on a couch next to mine so that his feet were touching my feet. He was under anesthesia, and my feet were touching his. Then they took me, did the appendectomy, and brought me back; I could not feel his feet anymore. In the morning, that old man died; and they took him, dead, away from my feet.

That was one encounter with the health system. My first experience, however, dates much earlier, when I was in the tenth grade. After the sophomore year, we all took an exam to continue into the eleventh grade, and all those who passed the exam were supposed to go and work at the Canal.[6] My father managed to get me out of it. He was working as an administrator at the Colentina Hospital, and he arranged for me to be hospitalized for ten days. I shared the ward with an older gentleman. People died there, too. But there was a huge "distance" between them and me: they were older. I had nothing in common with them.

My third encounter with a hospital was after *Stuff and Dough*, when I vomited blood and they took me to the ICU. It was very serious then; I thought I would die.

MF: An important figure in your films is that of the father who loses in power. I am thinking of *Stuff and Dough*, *Mr. Lazarescu*. . . .

CP: He loses his status as a father. It's the dark face of the father, of authority. For example, Marcel in *Stuff and Dough* or the doctors in *Mr. Lazarescu*.

MF: These examples undermine the father figure, the one who is supposed to make the law.

CP: Yes. This is the part where many atheists make a mistake when they argue that, if God exists, then why are there wars and suffering? . . . Such a way of thinking is the result of a misguided education, when one feels the need to admonish the parent, God the Father, who has created the world. I think this is a problem because people do not understand what it means to be a parent. If God were to intervene and eliminate all bad things, then he would be a parent who controls all the moments in your life. You would be completely annulled as an individual. In fact, the measure of a parent's wisdom and love for you is his gesture of giving you the freedom to act, a gesture that implies his own suffering. That is very important. I think that any discussion about God needs to start with an investigation into what God is, how he is, and what he means, and not with whether he exists or not.

MF: Can cinema encourage viewers to consider such questions? How do spectators relate to your films, in your opinion?

CP: I think that people who have indeed seen my films have seen a thing I have seen myself, and it is something that belongs to the ineffable, the unrepeatable. I'm referring to small fragments of things: a look, a just timing, a gesture, a word here and there . . . glimpses of the ineffable. That is all. Of course, for such glimpses to exist, it is necessary to have a solid construction that sustains them, that is, a story that makes some sense. [. . .]

One can say a lot of things about films, but very few people can talk about what is at the core of film X or Y because such analysis implies a very serious labor, a labor that you have to undertake yourself. The French have a saying: "se mettre à l'écoute," which means "putting oneself in the listening position." Listening is not a spontaneous act of the brain; one needs to set oneself in the condition of listening to the other, one needs to pay attention, to look at the world, that is, to rely on what one may call perception. David Bohm says something that I find very just: "Perception is an extension of the act of thinking."[7] Thinking is a process and our thoughts may prevent us from seeing the world. Bohm is right because the fabricated thought becomes a filter over one's eyes and one can no longer see the world . . .

MF: It becomes reality . . .

CP: Yes, it becomes a concrete object. Immaterial, but very concrete. And then one sees the world from the perspective of all types of thoughts or from the perspective of all types of authorities, whether these are called Shakespeare, Goethe, Hegel, Marx, or are represented by all sorts of ideologies that prevent one from seeing the world and from seeing the other. Who is the other? The other, the individual in front of us, has his or her own history that is not the same as the history of his or her group. . . . An individual's suffering is very personal and very much alive . . . so are his or her loneliness and fear. . . . It is difficult to reach these if one has all sorts of parasitical thoughts. If one takes the freedom to think and, as Bohm argues, to think of the relationship one has with the act of perception, then one can never reach ultimate, absolute conclusions. One is part of the world when thinking and being in the world are one, but that happens with only a few people or only for a few moments for most individuals. We *are not* in the world and, in fact, we keep choosing the outside position of observers; we observe, but we are not in tune with, we are not one with, the world.

MF: "Reality" is an elusive term. How do you see our relationship with whatever we call "reality"? What is "reality"?

CP: We do not know what "reality" is; it is, indeed, a question and it will remain as such. I do not think you can reach reality by means of words; I believe that any statement using words is approximate and very far away from what reality could be. I think that images, and all other nonverbal expressions of thought, related to anything, including reality, are as impotent as verbal discourse in making any valid claim about reality. I believe that, if there is anything we can call "reality," it cannot be expressed, but only lived. When I was studying painting, I was not fond at all of the "realist" painting of the nineteenth century (Courbet, Corot) or of Romanticism. To me, that period is a "black hole" in the history of art. (I am speaking especially about French painting). All the painters from Delacroix to Courbet do not interest me, do not move me, and do not produce any kind of reaction in me. Much more moving, and metaphysical, is, to me, the 1960–1970 American painting: photorealism or hyperrealism; I find it more elevated. While I was studying cinema in Geneva, I realized that I was very much interested in realism, but only in so far as it implies a possible meeting with the other, that is, a meeting with the world that is outside your own mind. In fact, I do not think that realism exists; it is merely a label. It is, rather, an administrative invention so that people do not get confused when they go into a bookstore or a library; we arrange books on a shelf according to labels: realism, surrealism, hyperrealism, symbolism, etc. I rather think that, if realism exists, then any artistic object belongs to this "trend." [. . .]

When I say that absolutely everything is "realistic," I mean that, presuming that there exists an objective reality beyond our own mind, there are two types of films: there are films in which the author's attention is primarily focused on what is taking place outside his or her own mind; that is observational cinema. Then there are films in which the author's attention falls on what is going on within his or her mind, and then we have all types of "realisms," from Aki Kaurismäki, Bresson, Antonioni, to films that belong to surrealism, and to the most extreme experiments. But an author's mind belongs to the real world, so when and how can one articulate a thought that is not "real"? Never. We are captive, in a good sense, in this world.

When I was interested in realism, I was getting increasingly interested in testimonials. If cinema is not a form of testimony, I am not interested in it. Not at all. A man is walking down a path—his life—and, while walking, he is talking to his fellow human beings about what he has found and what he has understood or not understood along the way, and the others do the same, so we have a dialogue. Dialogue and friendship are the most important things on earth; and both are inventions of our own minds. This is my own vision, at this particular moment, about the world and cinema.

The most complicated and difficult and extremely demanding thing in cinema is, therefore, to keep observation within the limits of the relationship you yourself have with the world, and not to intervene and "modify" the world in order to obtain certain effects that could produce I-don't-know-what special effects, that is, instead of looking at the world through a normal lens, to use a wide angle to create a specific effect and create a different screen for the viewer who was only eager to escape this world. I am quite interested in this "normalcy" . . . In fact, what do we call "normal"? What exactly do one's eyes see? Whose eyes? These kinds of questions preoccupy me and, while some may find such a preoccupation utopian, I am very interested in going away from any kind of convenient refuge that my mind might create.

MF: What role do stories and their structures play in *Aurora*?

CP: At the center of *Aurora* there is an erroneous reading of fairy tales; it is the story of a character who has misinterpreted fairy tales. He, then, decides to set the world in order, thinking that he has been, somehow, charged with a mission. What happens if we read stories verbatim? Well, this can happen.

MF: At the Cannes Film Festival, *Aurora* started with a scene in which Viorel is in bed with Gina. Why did you eliminate this scene when you released the film on DVD?

CP: I felt the scene was incomplete. The entire relationship between Viorel and Gina was changed by Clara Vodă, who did not do what I expected she would. In the script, her character, Gina, was a good, kind-hearted woman who was going through a suffering similar to Viorel's. Viorel is trying to "redo" his life in the same way that he is trying to "redo" his apartment, but his torment is so deep that it prevents him from finding his peace with Gina, who is there to save him; he passes by the woman who could have saved him. That would have been one sign of his affliction.

MF: *Aurora* is a film that pays very close attention to details.

CP: It is a film that relies on details. Everything has a meaning and I do believe that this is how things are. . . . The question is—and it is a very legitimate question that any individual has when encountering such situations—who the criminal is. The information that reaches us about criminals is negotiated by the media. There are a lot of interviews with all types of criminals, but, even then, the information is mediated by their own emotions and their own relationship with the universe. The judicial system collects information relevant to the case, but this is seldom revealing about the world of the criminal. Who is that man? What is his full identity, and not the one related only to statistics, IDs, birth certificates, etc.? In most cases, when somebody starts telling the story of a murderer, the narrative takes into account the final "result," i.e., that terrible event that is the murder. This is where the viewers of *Aurora* may be destabilized because they are forced, and, of course, they do not want, to reconsider the status, identity, and world of the murderer. For most of us, the murderer is, somehow, an individual who is, from the start, ready to kill, i.e., predestined to kill, but does not do it. For this reason, in most cases, films about murderers also have a therapeutic function because the viewer sees the murderer's behavior and says, "I do not behave like that, so that is not me. That one is bad and I am good." Somehow, one walks out of such films with some sense of self-satisfaction. The reality is a bit different, I believe, and I tried to build this man's story by giving up what the media or the police file might say about him. I tried to find out who this man is, what he wears, how he washes himself, eats, looks at things, does things we all do, things that I do or say. It was important that I play the role because it had to be a very personal rendering of the "events," a reenactment. If viewers understand this, then they also understand that the focus of the film is not the murder itself, that big event, but who this man is and what his journey is.

MF: One of the important questions the film seems to encourage is, "What is this man thinking about?"

CP: Yes. Such a thing is not recorded in any police files about him.

MF: Raymond Depardon has an interesting film, in this sense, *10ème chambre: Instants d'audience* (The 10th District Court: Judicial Hearings; 2004).

CP: Yes. He has another one titled *Délits fragrants* (Caught in the Acts; 1994).

MF: It's fascinating to observe people's reaction in front of the camera in his films.

CP: Yes. The camera-observer usually perverts the observed object, that is, people's behavior. People mistakenly believe that, once the camera is set in one place, it will record "reality"; in fact, the minute one places a camera in front of an individual, he or she will change his or her behavior in relationship with the observer for many reasons, some of which are completely mysterious. The most obvious ones may be called "survival instincts." People think that they are protecting themselves by providing a positive, bright image of who they are. I am interested in fictional cinema precisely because and when it can "deliver" one's intimate life; otherwise, I am not interested in it. One cannot "hunt" and film another one's intimate life with the help of a documentary device because people change their behavior. Fictional cinema, however, can construct it.

People are themselves in front of a camera when they are protected by a great love or when they have nothing to lose. Then marvelous things happen because they are blooming at that moment, very much alive.

Fiction allows me to construct people's intimate lives with the help of a number of instruments that, at the beginning, have nothing to do with the idea of authenticity, of truth, of recovering reality; one such instrument is the imagination, for example.

MF: How does imagination work?

CP: I often wonder what the imagination really is. What if it is, in fact, the faculty that generates possible worlds? What if it is merely an answer people have in their dialogue with the universe? Once a director makes a film that relies on his or her imagination and once the film is ready and on a screen, what if it becomes an answer to that director's indirect questions and an invitation to viewers to take part in this dialogue? Something like, "Here is the world as I can see it. . . ." What if viewers, upon seeing the film, experience a strong feeling, a sensation of having participated in something authentic? Then one can only conclude that imagination does not mean inventing situations that work out well, but, as in Plato's philosophy, it only means remembering certain things. I don't know. That's mere speculation. The imagination is not a game. The objects resulting from our imagination are deemed fictive in that they only exist within the limited realm of fiction. I don't think this is so. I think that, when you imagine certain things, you are, in fact, entering a dialogue with someone, I don't know with whom, and then you have your answers. Imagination is not spontaneous, anyway; you don't just push a button and you have your ideas. It is a continuous process: today you write something, but tomorrow you rewrite it or replace it with something else. It's as if you were experimenting with things when you are, in fact, connected to something beyond yourself. Primarily rational spirits make a mistake when they think that an individual is only in dialogue with himself or herself and, as a result, a work of art is born.

MF: What is the role of reason, then?

CP: Reason is a very serious instrument. It does not exist to comfort us, but to help us go beyond it. In your meeting with the world, it helps you more than you think. Most times, people adopt all sorts of formulas, and, when they do so, they abolish reason; it does not exist and it does not function anymore. You need some courage to put your own comfort at risk, and, throughout history, this has only happened to a few people—grand figures of history such as Giordano Bruno and

Galileo Galilei—about whom we know because their stories have been somehow passed down to us. If you really listen to your reason, you cannot end up in a position of total comfort, even if it first carries you there. That is only the beginning. You should have the courage to question, with the help of the same reason, the little "truths" you have acquired over time. That is difficult because you risk turning around in circles, like Hamlet, and abolishing any kind of action. There is that risk, yes. Rational thinking should necessarily guide one toward God. In fact, that is its major challenge.

Rational thinking, however, comes hand in hand with fear. Fear blocks everything; the fear of consequences blocks, in fact, your rational thinking. You discover something that is not in tune with what your community "sells" you about truth in this life; you discover something else. You need a bit of courage. Of course you may be mistaken, but a mistake can only be eliminated through dialogue. What I find grave and sad in today's world is that, having passed through so many murky times when people's thinking was limited by so many taboos, we are still trying to block rational thinking by imposing all sorts of taboos. We live in a world when we can hardly speak about many things. We are captives in our own fiction: that is the problem.

MF: What is the position of the camera, then? How does it mediate between the fictional world and the viewers?

CP: Yes, that is the question: what is the position of the camera? In cinema, in general. Where does one put the camera? David Mamet, in *On Directing Film,* writes that the director needs to know two things: what to tell the actors and where to place the camera. But here is the question: who is the one who is watching everything? It's a question that even older authors, be they playwrights or novelists, raised and it is an ever-present problem.

Whose point of view is it? For *Aurora,* the only formula I could find was to tell the cinematographer that the protagonist is watched by his father from heaven, that is, that the dead father is watching and cannot intervene. He can see everything, though. I was interested in a camera that had a worried gaze.

The camera is also fixed because we only have one point of view. If the camera-observer were to move in relation to the observed object, then it would create the illusion of multiple viewpoints, which is false.

The camera represents your cultural, emotional, intellectual acquisitions, that is, everything that you, the observer, are.

For *Mr. Lazarescu* I relied on long takes, but the camera was flexible and created the illusion of presence; this surprised me when I rewatched the film after a few years. From a philosophical point of view, I think it is, somehow, a form of deception, a lie. It is a lie because the camera creates the illusion of presence, of being there, when, paradoxically, the people who were physically around the dying man, were vaguely involved, uninvolved, indifferent, or aggressive toward him. The camera pays attention and comes and follows everything. False! It only creates the impression that it is present where it is not present; not only is it unable to do anything as an observer, but it also falsifies the discourse. It somehow "says" that you, the author, are "concerned." No kidding! If you are so concerned, put the camera down and go and help people in hospitals. That is the answer. You are not concerned, but you like it, and that is a very perverse form of wishful thinking that I have only realized some time later. At the time, I chose a flexible camera to be everywhere with that man. Yes, his fate did interest me, and it did hurt, and I did write this script out of revolt, but that is something else. What is the ideal position of the camera? Where could or should it have been placed? Why was the camera, that is, the observer, in other words, the author, more interested and involved, more engaged in the story than anybody else, even more than Mioara, the paramedic? Why was this position chosen? In cinema, the camera is the author. You cannot intervene in the story. It is only an illusion that we can intervene in things.

MF: Beyond its psychological and philosophical levels, *Aurora* also engages with the political aspects of life in a modern European capital. For example, in Pușa's apartment, which is also Viorel's childhood home, there are many old photos and old furniture.

CP: Old furniture and old hunting trophies. Here is the profile of Viorel's family, as I imagined it: Viorel was a child who had an unhappy, yet relatively comfortable, childhood. His father was some sort of a professor, but either a member of the Securitate or a collaborator. When I was young, the children who had those toy cars were the children of the Securitate "personnel." Those were Matchbox cars, and only people with money had them; at that time, people with money meant Securitate employees and the Party activists, those who had important positions.

MF: The ending of *Aurora* is quite reflexive about the creation process. Viorel is in the "spotlight," and the film seems to invite viewers to look at it as a "signature" film about an author.

CP: Yes. *Aurora* is also about the soft crimes whose authors we, the authors of films, books, poetry, and music, are. Articulating a discourse, imagining an object, and inventing, fabricating this object (be it a novel, a film, a poem, a symphony) presupposes a very acute consciousness of who you are. Whether you are wrong or not does not matter.

MF: It presupposes a form of violence . . .

CP: Yes. Because you also provoke a series of changes, even if very small, in the viewer's consciousness. And these are also small crimes. . . . When you "say" things, you "kill" them in the other, the recipient of your discourse. We all do these things in our daily lives, when we disappoint others and kill their expectations and hopes. I do not think it is a coincidence that we say the "author" of a crime and the "author" of a novel. I think this condition of the author needs to be investigated more. I think an author is the one who intervenes, brutally or not, in history.

MF: How difficult is it for you to make the next film?

CP: It is quite difficult because I have the vague sensation that there has been a radicalization of the discourse regarding cinema. For example, I think that we are being fooled by a certain identity of cinema that tends to be indivisibly connected to major events and then we have stories. Probably 80 to 90 percent of all films contain a mini-discourse about death, touch on death; if not, probably in 70 percent of the films, somebody dies, whether naturally, or assassinated. Furthermore, there are films about war and other major events important to a community. In films about smaller communities or families, somebody has to die, or give birth, or love and be betrayed. . . . If not, why make the film?

I think there must be a mistake in this approach to cinema. It's important for spectators to raise questions and engage with the film. If one can, for example, restore to viewers a Sunday with one's family when nobody dies, nobody gives birth, and there is no party and no wedding; if one can, for example, remake *Festen* (The Celebration; 1998) without the important revelation about the father, then can such a film work? I think it can. I think that the story of a Sunday with the family when nothing extraordinary happens can work; paradoxically, those things that the director can stage in an apartment will automatically speak of grand themes even if the director does not.[8] This is a question of a good management of the relationships among characters, of the rising and falling tensions among them. I believe this is essential in cinema and cinema can do it. I think that, today, the observational documentary can get very close to the intimate space or the inner life of the subject, and I think it is equal to fiction film, which is going in the same direction.

MF: I first saw *Three Exercises* at the Romanian Film Festival in New York. When the screening ended, I heard somebody behind me say, "What does this film have to do with Romanian cinema?"

CP: Because the film was in French and subtitled in English?

MF: Maybe. What "kind" of film is it?

CP: This is not an American film, if we were to judge by what we know about American cinema; it does not look like an American film. If we were to judge according to what we know about European cinema, a European cinema centered on the French tradition, we may easily say that it is European. The actors are French, it was shot in Toulouse, and it is dedicated to Eric Rohmer. I am not sure such a classification can help us, though.

MF: How would you describe European cinema?

CP: I have never thought of cinema in these terms. When I think, and speak, about cinema, I imagine it as a country to which all directors belong. When you get there, it is a territory, a "state" that functions only in reference to itself and where cultural differences are not important. These cultural differences exist, but in the way that cultural differences exist between two individuals belonging to the same nation: there are distinct voices. For example, French cinema has Rohmer, Godard, Truffaut: they are all distinct voices. Yes, they are all French and there are common things that unite them, but, in the same way, there are connections between, for instance, Rohmer's cinema and Jia Zhangke's or Abbas Kiarostami's. There are connections beyond these cultural differences, but I've never thought of art in these terms.

MF: How did the project for *Three Exercises* start?

CP: In 2008, Chantiers Nomades invited me to Grenoble to conduct a four-week workshop. About six months later, Frédéric Plazy, the director of the Chantiers Nomades, invited me to organize another workshop in Toulouse. I agreed.

In the morning, when I was packing my bags to leave for the airport, I saw Vladimir Solovyov's *Short Story of the Antichrist* on my table. I buy those books that have moved me in some way in many copies to give them to others, and I had about ten copies of this Solovyov book. I decided to take it. I know: it sounds like a joke, or like an American movie, but this is what really happened. I took two copies—one for Luchian Ciobanu, the cinematographer, with whom I was leaving—thinking that, on the plane, we will both read it and have an idea about what we would do. I was a bit excited by the idea that I was going to Cartesian France with a text about Jesus Christ and the existence of God. I thought this text would give birth to a lot of discussions.

MF: Solovyov's text is quite intricate. How did the actors react to it?

CP: There were many discussions. Each actor's background counted: for example, one was from the *banlieues*; another one was a practicing Catholic; a third was gay, and a fourth one was of Iranian-French descent and an atheist. People with very different histories and positions. Some even cried during our discussions. There are many underground meanings of Solovyov's text, and much of it is relevant today because the world has not changed too much since 1900.

MF: How did the "exercises" become a film?

CP: Once the workshop was over, I returned to Romania and I edited three distinct films to send them to the actors so that they could use them for their résumés. Sometime in August, the Romanian magazine *Dilema* organized a film festival in Alba-Iulia, and they asked me for *Aurora*. I offered to give them one of the *Three Exercises*. Mihai Chirilov, the programmer for the Transylvania International Film Festival, saw it there and he asked me for it, too; he wanted to release it on DVD, as a bonus for *Aperitiff*, the free magazine of the festival. I asked permission from the Chantiers Nomades, and they agreed. Evgeny Gusyatinskiy, one of the programmers for the Rotterdam International Film Festival, got a copy of the magazine, watched the film, and was eager to see the others. I edited all of them into one film, titled it *Three Exercises of Interpretation,* subtitled it, and sent it to Rotterdam. It was a tremendous work and Luchian Ciobanu helped me with it.

MF: Did the actors improvise, or did you give them a fully written text?

CP: They improvised. That was the purpose of the workshop. If I remember correctly, the title of the workshop was "Actor, Character, Author." Or something like that. During all our discussions there, before and during the making of the film, and, in fact, every time I am making a film, my priority is to persuade the actors to think like, and assume the role of, authors. While they are building or imagining the character, they need the director's help. To me, the ideal situation is that I remain only the director, a type of a "traffic sign," so to speak. I only "show" them where to go and where not to go, but I do not intervene in the actor's "kitchen" to tell them how to do it. When actors expect the director to tell them how to act, they are cowards. That is a very serious form of cowardice because, when the film is released, if it is successful, they, the actors-authors, would claim their rights over the characters they played.

MF: Who is the author of *Three Exercises*, then?

CP: We have Solovyov's text, so there is one author from the start. There are my intentions as a director. There are the characters, as imagined by the actors. All of these authors exist, not necessarily in this order of importance. But each of those asked to imagine, to build, to add a brick to film has a very serious responsibility.

MF: What was most important for all involved in this workshop?

CP: I am not sure that what was important to me was equally important to them. Two things were important to me: how a philosophical text can become a lively conversation today, and what the actor's contribution is in this situation. Acting means being present in the moment, and this necessitates courage. To be present then and there. I don't understand what talent is, but I do know what being present is and what it means to a film. I am convinced that, when people are present in front of the camera, I, the viewer, will watch them and listen to them, regardless of what they do or say because what matters is a certain vibration that characterizes life in action. The first enemy of this moment is the actor, whose inner censor keeps an eye on his or her actions. I am interested in making this censor disappear. . . . The meeting with an actor is, to me at least, only an opportunity to discover the human being within the actor, and the human being within me, as the director. I am interested in this human being; everybody is.

If acting makes any sense, then, to me this is it: acting is not a profession; it is a mission. The actor is the messenger of a higher truth, but, for this truth to take a form, the actor must give in. You know what they say: the believer does not have to think about what to say because he or she will open the mouth and God will speak through his or her words. The same happens to the actors when they assume the condition of missionaries.

There is a line in *The Mother and the Whore* when Jean-Pierre Léaud says, "To speak with somebody else's words"; that, I felt, was the ideal definition of acting because *you* are speaking, not who you think your character is. It is you who are speaking with somebody else's words. You take those words, you listen to them, you understand them, you listen to yourself and you use them as if you were living somebody else's life when, in fact, you are living your own life, but through somebody else's words. This is my own way of explaining, as clearly as I can, what I can only speculate about acting. I don't really know what happens when it works out. While making *Aurora,* I thought about things that had nothing to do with acting. First, I started each take with the sadness caused by the previous take and by my inability to communicate with my crew. Then, every time I had to get "into" the story and act, I started thinking of my father, my grandfather, and my childhood, trying to find, among my own memories, things that I had forgotten. . . . Acting as a form of self-knowledge: this is what I mean. Cinema gives actors this opportunity for self-knowledge.

MF: What do you believe are some of your challenges regarding filmmaking?

CP: I have my own obsessions about things that have to do with cinema, such as my inability to understand and use traveling shots, zooming, telephoto lenses, film music, and other similar strategies that deform reality. A story that lasts for more than twenty-four hours is very difficult for me because I cannot physically pull it off. The protagonist in *Aurora* does not sleep, which is how I could drag the plot on for two days. I think that the story made up of moments that the director deems important is a lie, especially when these moments are connected so well that they are "coherent." Does that really exist? I don't think so. I have a problem with that kind of cinema. I think cinema should be questioned every time.

MF: How did you get involved in the *Bridges of Sarajevo* project?

CP: This project, from what I know, was conceived by Mirsad Purivatra, the director of the Sarajevo Film Festival, and Jean-Michel Frodon, the former editor-in-chief of *Les Cahiers du Cinéma*, to commemorate one hundred years since the beginning of the First World War. Mirsad called me at the beginning of 2012, I think, to ask me whether I would be interested in participating in a collective project about Sarajevo. I told him I was interested, but I asked him for some time to think it over because it is not very difficult to become an impostor. Why would I say anything about Sarajevo? What exactly did I know about Sarajevo? After a few weeks, I had a certain story in mind, so I called Mirsad back. I said, "Yes, I am interested, but my story will be set in the present and the protagonists will be Romanians. I have been to Sarajevo only twice, and about Sarajevo I have learned from the history book, or from television, during the war in Yugoslavia, so I cannot really talk about the assault in more than approximate terms. I think I can say more about what is going on in the minds of some people in my country." He agreed with my proposal.

MF: What are the origins of your film's plot?

CP: Initially, the story was that of a couple of *nouveaux riches*, of a certain age, who are in Vienna to go to the Opera, like two authentic snobs. Having seen *The Gypsy Baron*, they start talking about differences, and people's reactions to differences, and to the other, in general. I had to change the plot for financial reasons, so, eventually, I decided to set it in the couple's bedroom in Romania. In the bedroom, people feel sheltered from everything and can say everything they can think of because there is no risk that what they say could turn against them.

Then I changed *The Gypsy Baron* for Herman Keyserling's book *Europe* (*Das Spektrum Europas*), which I had read some time at the beginning of the 1990s, when it was published in Romania. I have always found the first lines of the book, which the husband is reading in the film, very suggestive, "All nations are, of course, thoroughly unpleasant things. Man, as such, is a dubious enough sort of creature. Only in exceptional cases does a sample of the genus achieve the standards which everyone instinctively imposes on everyone else." This was the starting point; I used it to build the dialogue. . . . I thought that somehow, this sentence was not far from the truth. What he says, without being very philosophical about it, is that the demands we have towards others we don't have towards ourselves. Towards ourselves we are extremely tolerant.

It is also obvious to most Romanians that another source for this sketch was Ion Luca Caragiale's *Mr. Leonida Faces the Reactionaries:* the same situation, less glorious, though, and the same potential event (in Caragiale's play it is the beginning of Lent; in my film, it is New Year's Eve).

The initial title of my short was, in fact, "New Year's Eve"; I changed it to "Das Spektrum Europas" because I thought the Christmas tree was enough to mark the event. The intermittent gleaming of the tree lights also marks the discrepancies between what we know, what we think we know, and what we would like to know. Without having read the book, the husband makes some radical statements; he knows what it is about and he sends Keyserling to the corner. In her turn, the wife has not understood anything. They have enough education to be able to read in French, but they live in a world all to themselves. They each fabricate their own worlds.

What I was most interested in was the way in which we, people on Earth, march under all sorts of flags and claim that *our own* version of history is the right one. History is how *I* see it and as *I* know it. History is a long rubber band that everybody pulls in their direction, as they see fit. Yes, some events did take place, but they no longer exist; what we have is the story of these events. And this story is always complemented by its interpretation. I think it is healthier to assume your own share of guilt out of an event, to take a closer look at the beam in our own eye before we see the straw in somebody else's. That is why the film story had to be set in Romania.

In fact, this story could have happened anywhere: those two people could have been of any nationality. This tendency to fictionalize does not belong to only one nation or to only one culture; it belongs to all human beings. And not because human beings are necessarily interested in mystifying reality; quite the opposite, human beings are interested in restoring history, but this restoration, as long as it involves the speaker, will always be an approximate one.

Why would we mystify reality? I think that we are who we are, most of us, and that we end up thinking this way because we have not yet questioned how information is used, what this information means, and where and how we receive this information.

This is what happened to my generation when communism fell. History was retold in a different way. During communism, even if one questioned it, one often did it for economic reasons. If we had had enough food, if they had not cut the electric power, if we had had enough heat in the winter, if we had had enough television shows, probably people would not have come out in the streets. That is where the fundamental disagreement with the regime was for most of us; the dissidents had a completely different position.

I was twenty-two in 1989, and, like many others, I was interested in history, but I was raised a communist. I cried in the first grade, when they accepted me into the ranks of the Pioneers only in the second round; I believed in the cause of communism.[9] This indoctrination worked until I got into the eighth grade. At the age of fourteen, you somehow meet real life and, if you pay attention a little, you can see that things don't really work out. I saw that there were many things we could not say, that there was very serious censorship. . . . And these things went beyond the lack of food or electric power. If it hadn't been for the many things we could not do, we would not have questioned the history we were taught in school.

People of my generation, and those a bit younger, who were first taught one type of history and then learned of another, have kept, in my opinion, a keen interest for the ways in which history is told, regardless of what professions we have chosen. My interest in what history was and how it could be told expanded all of a sudden when I went through the 1990 events. After 1989, many books, including memoirs about the communist prisons, were published, and that moment completely destabilized and changed me. That was the real turn. Ceaușescu's fall made us happy, but it made us happy in that all of us who had been misinformed, manipulated, indoctrinated were waiting for a kind of [Mikhail] Gorbachev to come, and we all saw him in [Ion] Iliescu. I was discharged from the army on February 5, 1990, before the first elections on May 20. On February 6, I went to enroll in the Christian-Democratic National Peasants' Party, one of the historical parties that were reestablished after 1989; I had, by then, realized I was wrong about Iliescu.

During communism, we were told that these historical parties had oppressed the country. To a great extent, this was not untrue. What did these historical parties, which we so cherished immediately after 1990s, really mean? They were represented by a group of old men who had been through the communist prisons, and who had regained their lives, some in more dignified ways than others, after 1989. They were trying to tell us what life had been like before the communists. But, to be perfectly honest, even before the communists came, there had been many horrifying events, all happening while these historical parties were in power. It was a very confusing situation, but I did enroll in the party because, by then, I had managed to read a few interviews, a few books, and they opened my eyes to events I had never known about. I had not known that there was a Gulag in Romania. I did not know. I did not. I was interested in history, my parents were discussing things in the house, Radio Free Europe was talking about the inmates, but it all seemed so distant—an exception. I did not know that people were sent to these labor camps *en masse*. I did not know about the Piteşti Experiment.[10] I did not know about the entire network of political prisons: Gherla, Aiud, Sighet, Râmnicu Sărat, Mislea, the women's prison, the Canal. I did not know.

This is something that the critics of the New Romanian Cinema do not fully understand. There are critics who associate me with André Bazin. I heard of Bazin in school, and I read a few of his articles, but I never read *What Is Cinema?* in its entirety; I was not interested in it. I am a direct consequence of the communist system, of the fall of communism, of the University Square, and of everything that followed. I have had a direct, unmediated connection with History, with what it means, with the real, happening, history. And I reacted to it: I reacted to the lies. My cinema is not an intellectual pursuit. I never lived in an ivory tower; I went to the University Square and I screamed against communism until I got sore. The film I made during my third year in Geneva was based on one of Eugene O'Neill's one-act plays and it was titled *Before Breakfast*, but it was focused on my experience in the University Square.

It is impossible to recuperate—through words or images—what you have lived. Two years ago I discovered Arsenie Papacioc, who said one thing that surprised me: "Peace is more important than justice."[11] All these years, I kept thinking about peace and justice, and I have to admit he is right: yes, peace is more important than justice. I used to be convinced that, the minute justice was done, peace would follow.

No, peace never follows because justice is not possible; justice is only temporary. When justice is done, so to speak, one of the parties will always feel deceived. Things are very complicated and, unfortunately, our education does not focus on peace.

MF: What does cinema represent for you?

CP: The only thing that interests me about cinema, if I have to define it, is its capacity as a "mărturisire" (confession/testimony). When you give a testimony about something, it comes out very rough, not because you want it that way, but because, if you pay attention to what you are saying and eliminate all things that are improbable, what remains (those things that you remember) will line up in a very surprising manner that is quite cryptic for your listener. Out of nowhere, you build up certain obstacles and your listener cannot get to your story, that is, to what happened. *Paludes* (Marshlands; 1895) by André Gide, starts with, "*Avant d'expliquer aux autres mon livre, j'attend que d'autres me l'expliquent*" ("Before explaining my book to others, I'm waiting for the others to explain it to me"). Connected to his or her own memory, the director enters a relationship with the viewers. Hand in hand with them, and seated on a chair by them, the director watches his or her own film and a discussion begins. The director needs to be the equal of the viewers and to be the viewer of his or her own film.

MF: What role should cinema play in one's life?

CP: It continues to shock me that a high number of people—too high, in my opinion—take shelter in cinema and turn their backs on life. They cannot do such a thing. Cinema is only one other way of expressing a thought about life; it is as if one took refuge in a library. It's just as serious. This is, in fact, a paradox: you build your own universe and take refuge in it, and life does not matter to you anymore. That is a lie; it implies you are worshipping a wooden idol. Life is something else. Maybe that is why, when a regime is overthrown, intellectuals seem to be cowards. They don't understand another reality than the one in their own books. I don't think they should come out in the street, raise the flag, and be revolutionaries, but I think they should just denounce a lie. The most important function of an intellectual is to announce that the king is naked. They don't have to come out into the street, but they should not forget the distance between life and the representation of life they find in books or films.

Notes

The interview presented here is a condensed version of the much longer original conversation with the director. Part of this interview has been published as "Beyond the Real: An Interview with Cristi Puiu," *Studies in Eastern European Cinema* 5.2 (October 2014): 185–88.

1. In 2003, a number of young directors contested the results of the NCC selection process. Puiu was the only one who had received funds, but he was very vehement in his denunciation of what had happened.

2. Puiu does not include *Three Exercises* or *Sieranevada* in this number (the latter was not released at the time of this interview).

3. There is no connection between Ștefan and Emil Constantinescu; the surname is common in Romania.

4. ICECHIM is a research institute where Elena Ceaușescu used to be the manager. Ozana is one of Bucharest's neighborhoods.

5. Anca Puiu is Cristi Puiu's wife and the director of Mandragora, the couple's production company.

6. The "Canal" is the short for the Danube–Black Sea Canal, which was excavated with the help of political prisoners, students, and soldiers. Infamous as an extended labor camp in the 1950s, where many died in terrible conditions, the Canal was eventually finished in 1987.

7. David Bohm (1917–1992) was an American physicist especially known for his contribution to quantum theory.

8. Puiu's upcoming film *Sieranevada* is built around a family reunion when nothing "spectacular" happens.

9. At the age of seven or eight, students were enrolled in the lower ranks of the communist youth, the "Pioneers."

10. The Pitești Experiment, or Phenomenon, was conducted in the Pitești political prison, where young prisoners were submitted to a brainwashing technique to turn them into the torturers of the other prisoners.

11. Arsenie Papacioc (1914–2011) was an important monastic figure and religious philosopher in the Romanian Orthodox Church.

Filmography

13–19 iulie 1998, Craiova, Azilul de bătrîni (July 13th–July 19th 1998, Craiova, The Retirement Home; 1998)
Directors and Producers: Andreea Păduraru and Cristi Puiu
Director of Photography: Marius Panduru
Editors: Remus Stoica and Bogdan Gheorghe
Running time: 51 minutes
Cast: Andreea Păduraru, Katia Şalapă, Mihaela Deaconeci

Marfa şi banii (Stuff and Dough; 2001)
Production Company: Oficiul Național al Cinematografiei, S. C. Rofilm S. A., Studioul de Creație Cinematografică al Ministerului Culturii
Script: Cristi Puiu and Răzvan Rădulescu
Executive Producers: S. C. Rofilm S. A., Filmex—România
Director of Photography: Silviu Stavilă
Editor: Ines Barbu
Running time: 92 minutes
Cast: Alexandru Papadopol (Ovidiu), Dragoş Bucur (Vali), Ioana Flora (Betty), Luminița Gheorghiu (Mama), Răzvan Vasilescu (Marcel Ivanov), Doru Ana (Doncea), Costică Drăgănescu (Tatăl)

Un cartuş de Kent şi un pachet de cafea (Cigarettes and Coffee; 2004)
Production Company: Temple Film
Producer: Cristina Ionescu
Script: Cristi Puiu
Executive Producer: Dan Badea
Director of Photography: Oleg Mutu
Editor: Dana Bunescu
Running time: 13 minutes
Cast: Victor Rebengiuc (Mr. Tomescu), Mimi Brănescu (Vlad Tomescu), Mihai Brătilă (waiter)

Moartea domnului Lăzărescu (The Death of Mr. Lazarescu; 2005)
Production Company: Mandragora
Executive Producer: Alexandru Munteanu
Script: Cristi Puiu and Răzvan Rădulescu
Production Manager: Tudor Hristescu
Director of Photography: Oleg Mutu
Editor: Dana Bunescu
Running time: 153 minutes
Cast: Ioan Fiscuteanu (Mr. Lazarescu), Luminița Gheorghiu (Mioara Avram), Doru Ana (Sandu Sterian), Dana Dogaru (Mihaela "Miki" Sterian), Şerban Pavlu (Gelu), Gabriel Spahiu (Leo), Florin Zamfirescu (Dr. Ardelean), Bogdan Dumitrache (Medic), Dragoş Bucur (Mişu), Dan Chiriac (Medic), Clara Vodă (Gina Filip), Adrian Titieni (Dragoş Popescu), Mihai Brătilă (Dr. Breslaşu), Monica Bîrlădeanu (Mariana), Mimi Brănescu (Dr. Mirică), Rodica Lazăr (Dr. Laura Şerban), Alina Berzunțeanu (Dr. Zamfir), Simona Popescu (Nurse), Mirela Cioabă (Marioara)

Aurora (2010)
Production Company: Mandragora
Producers: Anca Puiu and Bobby Păunescu
Script: Cristi Puiu
Executive Producer: Anca Puiu
Director of Photography: Viorel Sergovici
Editor: Ioachim Stroe
Running time: 181 minutes
Cast: Cristi Puiu (Viorel Ghenghea), Clara Vodă (Gina Filip), Valeria Seciu (Puşa), Catrinel Dumitrescu (Rodica Livinski), Luminița Gheorghiu (Mioara Avram), Valentin Popescu (Doru), Gelu Colceag (Dan Livinski), Ion Stoica (Ploscaru), Conastantin Diță (the detective)

Trois exercices d'interprétation (Three Exercises of Interpretation; 2011)
Production Companies: Chantiers Nomades and Mandragora
Script: Cristi Puiu and Vladimir Solovyov
Director of Photography: Luchian Ciobanu
Running time: 157 minutes
Cast: Marion Bottollier, Patrick Vaillant, Ugo Broussot, Jean-Benoît Poirier, Anne-Marie Charles, Ludivine Anbérrée, Diana Sakalauskaite, Barnabé Perrotey, Hillary Keegin, Perrine Guffroy, Anne Courpron, Nathalie Meunier

"Das Spektrum Europas" (2014)
Production Companies: Obala Art Centar, deFilm, Digital Cube
Producers: Mirsad Purivatra, Izeta Gradjević, Jovan Marjanović
Script: Cristi Puiu

Director of Photography: Luchian Ciobanu
Editor: Ioachim Stroe
Cast: Marian Râlea (Mr. Popescu), Valeria Seciu (Mrs. Popescu)

Bibliography

"4 Months, 3 Weeks, 2 Days." *Box Office Mojo,* n.d.; accessed April 15, 2015. http://www.boxofficemojo.com.

Aguilar, Gonzalo. *Other Worlds: New Argentine Films*. Trans. Sarah Ann Wells. New York: Palgrave Macmillan, 2008.

Andrew, Dudley. "The Unauthorized Auteur Today." In *Film and Theory: An Anthology*. Edited by Robert Stam and Toby Miller. Malden, Mass.: Blackwell Publishers, 2000. 20–31.

Ash, Timothy Garton. "Eastern Europe: The Year of Truth." *New York Review of Books,* February 15, 1990; accessed September 21, 2014. http://www.nybooks.com.

———. "Ten Years After." *New York Review of Books,* November 18, 1999; accessed September 25, 2014. http://www.nybooks.com.

Associated Press. "Sarajevo: The Slaying That Set Off World War I." *New York Times,* June 19, 2014; accessed June 5, 2014. http://www.nytimes.com.

Astruc, Alexandre. "The Birth of a New Avant-Garde: La Caméra-Stylo." In *The New Wave*. Ed. Peter Graham. Garden City, N.Y.: Doubleday, 1968. 17, qtd. in Alan Williams. *Republic of Images*. 306.

"Aurora." MEDIA Film Database, n.d.; accessed March 30, 2015. http://www.mfdb.eu.

Bachman, Ronald D., ed. *Romania: A Country Study*. Washington, D.C.: GPO for the Library of Congress, 1989; accessed September 28, 2014. http://countrystudies.us.

Bălan, Mira. "Țară fără vinovați: Cazul Nica după nouă ani." *Jurnalul national,* April 13, 2006; accessed March 4, 2015. http://jurnalul.ro.

Bardan, Alice. "Corneliu Porumboiu's 12:08 East of Bucharest (2006) and Romanian Cinema." In *A Companion to Eastern European Cinemas.* Ed. Anikó Imre. Malden, Mass.: Wiley-Blackwell, 2012. 125–47.

Bardem, Juan Antonio. "Report on the Current State of Our Cinema." In *Death of a Cyclist*. Criterion Collection DVD booklet. Ed. Elizabeth Helfgot. Trans. Mariana Carreño King. Criterion, 2008. 22–24.

Baudrillard, Jean. "The Timisoara Massacre." In *The Illusion of the End*. Trans. Chris Turner. Stanford, Calif.: Stanford University Press, 1994 54–61.

Blaga, Iulia. "*Aurora* Winds Up Postproduction." *Film New Europe,* March 11, 2010; accessed March 30, 2015. http://web.archive.org.

———. "Mare triumph românesc—Cristi Puiu ia Ursul de Aur pentru scurt metraj." *România liberă,* 2004. *LiterNet*, February 2004; accessed February 26, 2015. http://agenda.liternet.ro.

Bohlen Celestine. "Romanian Miners Invade Bucharest." *New York Times,* June 15, 1990; accessed September 25, 2014. http://www.nytimes.com.

Boia, Lucian. *De ce e România altfel?* 2nd ed. Bucharest: Humanitas, 2013.

———. *History and Myth in Romanian Consciousness*. Budapest: Central European University Press, 2001.

———. *România, țară de frontieră a Europei.* Bucharest: Humanitas, 2012.

Bordwell, David. "Parametric Narration." In *Narration in the Fiction Film.* Madison: University of Wisconsin Press, 1985. 274–311.

"The Bridges of Sarajevo." *Bridgesofsarajevo.com,* n.d.; accessed June 8, 2015. http://bridgesofsarajevo.com.

Brooke, Michael. "The Death of Mr. Lazarescu." *Sight and Sound* 16.8 (August 2006): 68–70.

Brown, John Murray, et al. "Daunted by Deficits." *Financial Times,* June 23, 2010; accessed June 5, 2015. www.ft.com.

Bruno, Giuliana. *Atlas of Emotion.* New York: Verso, 2002.

Bucur, Dragoș. "RetrospecTIFF (1): Dragoș Bucur: 'Da, și eu trăiesc din actorie!" Interview by Mihnea Măruță. *Surpriza lui Mihnea Măruță,* June 17, 2011; accessed January 24, 2015. http://mihneamaruta.ro.

———. "'Un rol bun e acela în care personajul e vulnerabil.'" Interview by Svetlana Cârstean. *Observatorul cultural* 145 (December 2002); accessed May 6, 2015. http://www.observatorcultural.ro.

Căliman, Călin. *Istoria filmului românesc: 1897–2010.* Bucharest: Asociația Contemporanul, 2011.

"Cannes Boost for 'Bridges of Sarajevo.' " *Euronews,* May 30, 2014; accessed June 6, 2015. http://www.euronews.com.

Cârneci, Magda. *Artele plastice în România 1945–1989. Cu o addenda 1990–2010.* Iasi, Romania: Polirom, 2013.

Chatman, Seymour. "The Cinematic Narrator." In *Film Theory and Criticism: Introductory Readings.* Eds. Leo Braudy and Marshall Cohen. 5th ed. New York and Oxford: Oxford University Press, 1999. 473–87.

Chirilov, Mihai, and Ana Maria Sandu. "Hot Stuff." *Aperitiff* (2011): 50–56.

Colegiul Medicilor din România. "Declarația Consiliului Național al Colegiului Medicilor din România." *Cmr.ro,* September 5, 2015; accessed January 9, 2016. http://www.cmr.ro.

"Concurs proiecte cinematografice sesiunea I 2008." Centrul Național al Cinematografiei, June–July 2008; accessed July 28, 2015. http://cnc.gov.ro.

Constantinescu, Emil. *Păcatul originar, sacrificiul fondator: Revoluția din '89 așa cum a fost*. Bucharest: Minerva, 2009.

Cowell, Alan. "On Centenary of World War I, Europe Sees Modern Parallels." *New York Times,* August 4, 2014; accessed June 5, 2015. http://www.nytimes.com.

"Crestem spaga ca sa nu murim in spitale?" *Ziare.com,* February 6, 2009; accessed March 4, 2015. http://www.ziare.com.

Day, Matthew. "'Romania's Nuremberg' Begins with Prison Camp Commandant." *The Telegraph,* September 24, 2014; accessed March 30, 2015. http://www.telegraph.co.uk.

"The Death of Mr. Lazarescu." *Box Office Mojo,* n.d.; accessed March 13, 2015. http://www.boxofficemojo.com.

Decret-Lege nr. 80 (February 8, 1990): Art. 5. Romanian Government. 1990. *Cauta Lege*, n.d.; accessed July 25, 2012. http://www.cautalege.ro.

De Vos, Susan, and Gary Sandefur. "Elderly Living Arrangements in Bulgaria, the Czech Republic, Estonia, Finland, and Romania." *European Journal of Population* 18.1 (2002): 21–38.

Deletant, Dennis. *Romania under Communist Rule*. 2nd ed. Bucharest: Civic Academy Foundation, 2006.

"Diagnostic Surveys of Corruption in Romania." World Bank, March 29, 2001; accessed March 9, 2015. http://www1.worldbank.org.

"Distribution support—year 2010." EURIMAGES—European Cinema Support Fund, Council of Europe, n.d.; accessed March 30, 2015. http://www.coe.int.

Djilas, Milovan. *The New Class: An Analysis of the Communist System.* New York and Washington: Frederick A. Praeger Publishers, 1966.

Dumitrescu, Laura. "Cristi Puiu—*non so se s'è la desiata luce*." In *Politicile filmului: Contribuții la interpretarea cinemaului românesc contemporan*. Eds. Andrei Gorzo and Andrei State. Cluj-Napoca, Romania: Tact, 2014. 27–47.

Dumitrescu, Mircea. *O privire critică asupra filmului românesc.* Brasov, Romania: Arania, 2005.

"După șase ani. Ce cred românii despre Uniunea Europeană"? Institutul Român pentru evaluare și strategie, May 8, 2013; accessed June 5, 2015. http://www.ires.com.ro.

Eliade, Mircea. *The Sacred and the Profane: The Nature of Religion*. Trans. Willard R. Task. New York: Harcourt, Brace & World, 1959.

Elsaesser, Thomas. *European Cinema: Face to Face with Hollywood.* Amsterdam: Amsterdam University Press, 2005.

EURIMAGES—European Cinema Support Fund. Council of Europe, n. d.; accessed October 3, 2014. http://www.coe.int.

Ferencz-Flatz, Christian. *Incursiuni fenomenologice în noul film românesc*. Cluj-Napoca, Romania: Tact, 2015.

"Film List: Country: Romania." MEDIA Film Database, n.d.; accessed March 30, 2015. http://www.mfdb.eu.

"FIPRESCI Awards." 42nd International Thessaloniki Film Festival, November 9–18, 2001; accessed January 24, 2015. http://www.filmfestival.gr.

Flora, Ioana. "Interviu cu actrița Ioana Flora—'Am crescut printre oameni mari.'" Interview. *Elle Romania,* May 24, 2012; accessed May 6, 2015. http://www.elle.ro.

"Funding History." EURIMAGES—European Cinema Support Fund, Council of Europe, n. d.; accessed March 30, 2015. http://www.coe.int.

Gaidenko, Piama. "Solovyov, Vladimir Sergeevich (1853–1900)." In *Encyclopedia of Philosophy*. Ed. Donald M. Borchet. 2nd ed. Vol. 9. Detroit: Macmillan Reference, 2006. 122–27. Gale Virtual Reference Library; accessed January 10, 2016. http://go.galegroup.com.

Galt, Rosalind. *The New European Cinema: Redrawing the Map.* New York: Columbia University Press, 2006.

Geertz, Clifford. "Toward an Interpretive Theory of Culture." In *The Interpretation of Cultures: Selected Essays*. New York: Basic Books, 2000. 3–30.

Gilbey, Ryan. "Chasing the Ambulance." *Sight and Sound* 16.8 (August 2006): 28–30.

Gledhill, John, and Charles King. "Romania since 1989: Living beyond the Past." In *Central and East European Politics: From Communism to Democracy*. 2nd ed. Eds. Sharon L. Wolchik and Jane L. Curry. Lanham, Md.: Rowman and Littlefield, 2011. 313–35.

Gorzo, Andrei. "Top 5—Scurt circuit." *LiterNet.ro. Dilema veche* (July 2004); accessed February 26, 2015. http://agenda.liternet.ro.

———. *Lucruri care nu pot fi spuse altfel: Un mod de a gândi cinemaul de la André Bazin la Cristi Puiu*. Bucharest: Humanitas, 2012.

Grimshaw, Anna, and Amanda Ravetz. *Observational Cinema: Anthropology, Film, and the Exploration of Social Life.* Bloomington and Indianapolis: Indiana University Press, 2009.

Gurescu, George. "Memorialul durerii." *Televiziunea română*, n.d.; accessed October 13, 2014. http://www.tvrplus.ro.

Gusejnova, Dina. "Noble Continent? German-Speaking Nobles as Theorists of European Identity in the Interwar Period." In *Europe in Crisis. Intellectuals and the European Idea, 1917–1957*. Eds. Mark Hewitson and Matthew D'Auria. Oxford and New York: Berghahn, 2012. 111–33.

Havel, Václav. "The Power of the Powerless." In *The Power of the Powerless: Citizens against the State in Central-Eastern Europe*. Ed. John Kean. London and Melbourne: Hutchinson, 1985. 23–96.

Henley, Jon. "Europe's Leaders Hail Ties of Peace as They Mark First World War Centenary." *The Guardian,* August 4, 2014; accessed June 5, 2015. http://www.theguardian.com.

Hill, Steven. "A Two-Tier EU Is Preferable to David Cameron's 'In or Out' Vote." *The Guardian,* January 29, 2013; accessed June 5, 2015. http://www.theguardian.com.

Hirsch, Marianne. *Family Frames: Photography Narrative and Postmemory.* Cambridge, Mass., and London: Harvard University Press, 1997.

"The History of the European Union." European Union, n.d.; accessed June 4, 2015. http://europa.eu.

Hoberman, J. *Film After Film Or, What Became of 21st Century Cinema?* London and New York: Verso, 2012.

Hockenos, Paul. "World War I Conference in Sarajevo Divides Scholars." *New York Times,* June 22, 2014; accessed June 5, 2014. http://www.nytimes.com.

Holden, Stephen. "In a Modern Hospital Tale, Only Death Has Patience." *New York Times,* April 26, 2006; accessed March 20, 2015. http://www.nytimes.com.

Hughes, Kirsty. "Analysis: An EU of Two Tiers after Eurozone Debt Crisis." *BBC*. British Broadcasting Corporation, October 28, 2011; accessed June 5, 2015. http://www.bbc.com.

Ianoși, Ion. "Studiu introductiv." In Vladimir Solovyov. *Povestire despre Antichrist*. Trans. Dana Cojocaru. Bucharest: Humanitas, 2005. 5–24.

Imre, Anikó. "Eastern European Cinema from *No End* to the End (As We Know It)." In *A Companion to Eastern European Cinemas*. Ed. Anikó Imre. Malden, Mass.: Wiley-Blackwell, 2012. 1–23.

———. "Global Media and National Value: Postsocialist Negotiations." In *Postcommunism, Postmodernism, and the Global Imagination*. Ed. Christian Moraru. New York: Columbia University Press, 2009. 231–50.

"Istoric." Centrul Național al Cinematografiei Romania, n. d.; March 4, 2015. http://cnc.gov.ro.

"Jan 22, 2004: Giving All for a Genre: The Short Film Competition Is Complete." Press Releases 2004. Berlin International Film Festival, January 22, 2004; accessed January 26, 2015. https://www.berlinale.de.

Jaspers, Karl. *The Question of German Guilt*. Trans. E. B. Ashton. New York: Capricorn Books, 1961.

Judt, Tony. *Postwar: A History of Europe since 1945*. New York: Penguin Books, 2005.

Keyserling, Hermann. *Europe (Das Spektrum Europas)*. London: Jonathan Cape, 1928.

Korzybski, Alfred. "The World Is NOT an Illusion." Streaming by Gabriel Carvalho. YouTube, September 27, 2012; accessed January 10, 2016. http://www.youtube.com.

Kotkin, Stephen. *Uncivil Society: 1989 and the Implosion of the Communist Establishment.* New York: Modern Library, 2010.

"La CEDH condamne la Roumanie vingt-quatre ans après la répression de manifestations." *Le Monde,* September 17, 2014; accessed September 25, 2014. http://www.lemonde.fr.

Lefebvre, Henri. *The Production of Space*. Trans. Donald Nicholson-Smith. Malden, Mass.: Blackwell Publishing, 1991.

Lungu, Adrian. "Increderea in UE la romani—dupa modelul increderii in biserica." *EurActiv.ro,* July 9, 2008; accessed June 4, 2015. www.euractiv.ro.

"MAI 2015—Atitudinile românilor față de Uniunea Europeană și parcursul European al Republicii Moldova." INSCOP Research, April 30, 2015; accessed June 5, 2015. http://www.inscop.ro.

Mamet, David. *True and False: Heresy and Common Sense for the Actor.* New York: Pantheon Books, 1997.

Marinov, Laurențiu. "Scandalul muribundului plimbat între spitale produce o anchetă." *Șansa buzoiană* 4748 (July 18, 2014); accessed March 4, 2015. http://www.sansabuzoiana.ro.

Mazierska, Ewa. "The Redundant Male: Representations of Masculinity in Polish Postcommunist Cinema." *Journal of Film and Video* 55.2–3 (Summer/Fall 2003): 29–43.

MEDIA Programme (2007–2013). European Commission, n.d.; accessed March 30, 2015. http://ec.europa.eu.

Mitchievici, Angelo. "Filmul românesc după 1989: radiografia unei iluzii." In *Filmele care ne-au schimbat viața.* Cluj-Napoca, Romania: Eikon, 2013. 41–63.

Mototolea, Marius. "Un bărbat a murit după ce a fost 'plimbat' între spitalele Tecuci-Focșani-Galați." *Adevărul,* October 23, 2012; accessed March 4, 2015. http://adevarul.ro.

Nasta, Dominique. *Contemporary Romanian Cinema: The History of an Unexpected Miracle.* London and New York: Wallflower Press, 2013.

Neagu, Alina. "Eurobarometru: Increderea romanilor in Uniunea Europeana, la cel mai scazut nivel." *Hot News,* April 3, 2012; accessed June 5, 2015. http://www.hotnews.ro.

Nietzsche, Friedrich. "From On Truth and Lie in an Extra-Moral Sense." In *The Portable Nietzsche.* Trans. Walter Kaufmann. New York: Penguin Books, 1954. 42–47.

Perețianu, Dan. "Onorariile, șpaga și salariile medicilor." *Viața medicală* 46 (November 13, 2015); accessed January 9, 2016. http://www.viata-medicala.ro.

Perlez, Jane. "Romania's Anti-communist Revolutionary." *New York Times,* November 19, 1996; accessed September 25, 2015. http://www.nytimes.com.

Péron, Didier. "La Roumaine cuite al 'Dante'." *La Libération,* January 11, 2006; accessed March 13, 2015. http://next.liberation.fr.

Pîrvulescu, Cristian. "Regăsirea Europei?" *Observatorul cultural* 721 (May 2014); accessed June 4, 2015. http://www.observatorcultural.ro.

Pop, Doru. *Romanian New Wave: An Introduction.* Jefferson, N.C.: McFarland, 2014.

Popescu, Cristian Tudor. *Filmul surd în România mută: politică și propagandă în filmul românesc de ficțiune (1912–1989).* Iasi, Romania: Polirom, 2011.

Pricop, Lucian. *Managementul producției de film.* Bucharest: Tritonic Academic Books, 2011.

Puiu, Cristi. "An Interview with Cristi Puiu." Interview by Mihnea Măruță. In *Tribute to Cristi Puiu.* Sarajevo: Sarajevo Film Festival, 2013. 5–15.

———. "Critics' Talk #1: Cristi Puiu (*Trois exercices d'intepr étation*)." Interview by Nausicaa Marbe. YouTube.com. Streaming by International Film Festival Rotterdam, January 25, 2013; accessed May 20, 2015. https://www.youtube.com.

———. "Interview with Cristi Puiu." Interview by Kostanty Kuzma and Moritz Pfeifer. *East European Film Bulletin* (July 1, 2011); accessed December 20, 2015. *https://eefb.org*.

———. "Interviu Cristi Puiu 2015." Interview by Cristina Corciovescu. You Tube Streaming by All About Romanian Cinema, June 21, 2015; accessed December 21, 2015. https://www.youtube.com.

———. "'Cineva trebuie să plătească pentru ce s-a intâmplat la CNC': Dialog cu Cristi Puiu." Interview by Ovidiu Șimonca. *Observatorul cultural* 355 (January 2007); accessed January 24, 2015. http://www.observatorcultural.ro.

———. "Cristi Puiu despre cum a luat nastere filmul 'Aurora'." Interview. *You Tube*. Streaming by Atovidiu, May 15, 2010; accessed April 3, 2015. https://www.youtube.com.

———. "Every Film Must Be an Exercise: Cristi Puiu on *Three Interpretation Exercises*." Interview by Aaron Cutler. *Cinema Scope* 55 (Summer 2013); accessed May 6, 2015. http://cinema-scope.com.

———. "Keyserling la Sarajevo: Motivație regizorală." Message to the author. July 10, 2013. Email.

———. "Manifest împotriva operei inventate din nimic." Interview by Valerian Sava. In *O istorie subiectivă a tranziției filmice: Al Patrulea Val, restaurația mediocrată și refondarea cinemaului românesc*. Vol. 1. Pitesti, Romania: Paralela 45. 96–103.

———. "Murder in Mind." Interview by Nick James. *Sight and Sound* 22.12 (December 2012): 40–43.

———. "*Sieranevada*: intenție regizorală." Message to the author. April 1, 2015. 1–3. Email.

Quandt, James. "As He Lay Dying: James Quandt on *The Death of Mr. Lazarescu*." *Artforum International* 44.8 (April 2006): 81–82.

Quinn, Ben Antoine Reverchon, Raffaello Masci, and Dr Joachim Käppner. "First World War: How Countries across Europe Will Mark Centenary." *The Guardian*, January 16, 2014; accessed June 5, 2015. http://www.theguardian.com.

Radu, Raluca-Nicoleta. *Instituții culturale în tranziție: despre creativitate în journalism și cinematografia din România după 1944*. Bucharest: Nemira Publishing House, 2011.

Rațiu, Dan Eugen. *Disputa modernism-postmodernism: O introducere în teoriile contemporane asupra artei*. 2nd ed. Cluj-Napoca, Romania: Eikon, 2012.

"Results of the 2013 European Elections: Seats by Political Group and Member State." European Parliament, n.d.; accessed June 5, 2015. http://www.europarl.europa.eu.

Riding, Alan. "Failure May Be Cruel, but Success Can Be Sickening." *New York Times*, April 23, 2006; accessed March 4, 2015. http://www.nytimes.com.

Roman, Denise. *Fragmented Identities: Popular Culture, Sex, and Everyday Life in Postcommunist Romania*. Lantham, Md., Boulder, Colo., and New York: Lexington Books, 2007.

Sava, Valerian. "Falimentul cinematografiei buftene și sfîrșitul criticii cameleonice." *România literară* 35 (1999); accessed October 13, 2014. http://www.romlit.ro.

———. *O istorie subiectivă a tranziției filmice: Al Patrulea Val, restaurația mediocrată și refondarea cinemaului românesc*. 3 vols. Pitesti, Romania: Paralela 45, 2011–2013.

Șerban, Alex. Leo. "Bridging the Gap: Where Does the Romanian New Wave Go from Here?" *Film Comment* 47.1 (2011): 12–13.

———. *De ce vedem filme: Et in Arcadia Cinema*. Iasi, Romania: Polirom, 2006.

———. *4 decenii, 3 ani și 2 luni cu filmul românesc*. Iasi, Romania: Polirom, 2009.

Șerban, Alex. Leo, and Mihai Chirilov. "*Stuff and Dough*: Then. . . ." *Aperitiff* (2011): 54–56.

Șerban Alex. Leo, and Andrei Gorzo. "Critica de stânga față cu 'reacțiunea' din cinema—dialog între Alex. Leo Șerban și Andrei Gorzo." *Dilema Veche*, December 3, 2010; accessed December 19, 2015. http://dilemaveche.ro.

"Situația numărului de spectatori înregistrați de filmele românești ieșite în premieră până la 31.12. 1989." Centrul Național al Cinematografiei, December 31, 1997; accessed September 28, 2014. https://www.yumpu.com.

Sklar, Robert. "The Death of Mr. Lazarescu." *Cineaste* 31. 3 (Summer 2006): 62–63.

Sobchack, Vivian. *The Address of the Eye: A Phenomenology of Film Experience*. Princeton, N.J.: Princeton University Press, 1991.

Solovyov, Vladimir. *War, Progress, and the End of History: Three Conversations Including a Short Story of the Anti-Christ*. Trans. Alexander Bakshy. Hudson, N.Y.: Lindisfarne Press, 1990.

Sontag, Susan. *Regarding the Pain of Others*. New York: Picador, 2004.

Standing, Guy. *The Precariat: The New Dangerous Class*. London: Bloomsbury Academic, 2011.

Steefel, Lawrence D., Jr. "A Neglected Shadow in Poussin's *Et In Arcadia Ego*." *Art Bulletin* 57.1 (1975): 99–101.

Suciu, Oana-Valentina. "Migration and Demographic Trends in Romania: A Brief Historical Outlook." *Proceedings of the Center for Research into Post-Communist Economies 2010 Colloquium, Part II: Migration in Europe—Romania* (2010): 1–32; accessed September 25, 2014. http://www.crce.org.uk.

Thompson, James. "Nicolas Poussin." *The Metropolitan Museum of Art Bulletin* 50. 3 (Winter 1992–1993): 3–56.

Tismaneanu, Vladimir. *Stalinism pentru eternitate: O istorie politică a comunismului românesc*. Trans. Cristina Petrescu and Dragoș Petrescu. Bucharest: Humanitas, 2014.

Traynor, Ian. "2014: A Rough Year for Europe, with Worse to Come." *The Guardian*, December 31, 2014; accessed January 5, 2015. http://www.theguardian.com.

———. "Greece to Face Ultimatum from Eurozone and IMF." *The Guardian*, June 2, 2015; accessed June 5, 2015. http://www.theguardian.com.

Tuca, Marius. "5. 05. 2003—Despre incalzirea globala si scandal in cinematografie." *Marius Tuca Show. Antena* 1 (May 5, 2003). YouTube.com. Streaming by mariustucashow, February 24, 2012; accessed February 12, 2015. www.youtube.com.

Uricaru, Ioana. "Follow the Money: Financing Contemporary Cinema in Romania." In *A Companion to Eastern European Cinemas*. Ed. Anikó Imre. Malden, Mass.: Wiley-Blackwell, 2012. 427–53.

Varendoe, Kirk. "Minimalism and After." *MOMA* 4.1 (January 2001): 2–5.

Verdery, Katherine. *What Was Socialism and What Comes Next?* Princeton, N.J.: Princeton University Press, 1996.

Vodă, Eugenia. "Cannes—Maradona la filmul lui Cristi Puiu." *Jurnalul National*, May 22, 2005; accessed July 5, 2015.http://jurnalul.ro.

Weissberg, Jay. "Cannes Film Review: 'The Bridges of Sarajevo.'" *Variety*, May 30, 2014; accessed June 6, 2015. http://variety.com.

Williams, Alan. *Republic of Images: A History of French Filmmaking*. Cambridge, Mass.: Harvard University Press, 1992.

Wolff, Janet. "The Meaning of Minimalism." *Contexts* 4.1 (Winter 2005): 65–68.

Wollen, Peter. "The Auteur Theory." In *Film and Theory: An Anthology*. Eds. Robert Stam and Toby Miller. Malden, Mass.: Blackwell Publishers, 2000. 519–35.

World Health Organization. *The World Health Report 2006: Working Together for Health*. Geneva: World Health Organization, 2006; accessed January 9, 2016. http://www.who.int.

"World Premiere of 'Bridges of Sarajevo' at Cannes Film Festival." Sarajevo Film Festival, May 22, 2014; accessed June 8, 2015. http://www.sff.ba.

Žižek, Slavoj. *Violence: Six Sideways Reflections*. New York: Picador, 2008.

Index

Bold page numbers indicate Puiu films in filmography.

Akerman, Chantal, 4, 82
Allio, René, 74
Amen (2002), 24
Ana, Doru, 40–42, 61, 151, 152
Anbérrée, Ludivine, 100, 102–3, 152
Andrew, Dudley, 96
antihero/ "redundant male," 76–79, 82–83, 85, 90–91
anti-Semitism, 13, 112
Antonescu, Ion, 24
Antonioni, Michelangelo, 133
Aperitiff (magazine), 141
The Archive of Pain (2000), 4, 127–28
The Arrival of a Train at La Ciotat Station (1895), 95
Ash, Timothy Garton, 17, 18, 21
Astruc, Alexandre, 91
Atlas of Emotion (Bruno), 30
Aurora (2010), 60, 72–96, 116, 133–35, 139, 141, **152**; authorship and, 90–96; camera work, 80–81, 84, 86–90, 93–94, 137; at Cannes Film Festival, 85, 134; death and violence in, 8, 12, 75–78, 81–83, 85–90, 92, 134–35, 138–39; documentary-style approach in, 2, 74–75; ethnographic "thick description" (Geertz) in, 83; fathers and sons/male characters, 74–75, 78, 83–85, 89–90; female characters, 85–87; funding issues, 125; gaps in narrative, 68; political aspects of life, 138–39; "precariat"/capitalism in, 75–80; Puiu as cast member, 72–96, 143, 152; "redundant male"/antihero in, 76–79, 82–83, 85, 90–91; in *Six Tales from the Outskirts of Bucharest* series, 74; stories and structures in, 133–35; summary, 12, 74–75; web of obscure relationships, 82–84; withdrawal into memory, 87–89
auteur cinema, 16–17, 95–96
authorship, 90–96; *auteurs* and, 95–96; *camera-stilo* (camera-pen), 91, 94–95; "cinematic narrator" *versus* author, 92–95; "detached introspection," 93–95; recognition in, 96–98

Badea, Dan, 151
Bălan, Mira, 60
Barbu, Ines, 151
Bardan, Alice, 74
Bardem, Juan Antonio, 27
Bartas, Sarūnas, 106
Baudrillard, Jean, 19
Bazin, André, 4, 5, 147
Before Breakfast (O'Neill), 147
Before Breakfast (Puiu student film), 147
Begic, Aida, 108
Berlin International Film Festival, 50–51, 58, 59, 96–97
Berzunțeanu, Alina, 152
Beyond the Hills (2012), 97
Bîrlădeanu, Monica, 152
Blaga, Iulia, 58, 73
Bohlen, Celestine, 20
Bohm, David, 102, 131–32, 149n7

Boia, Lucian, 10, 13–14, 15, 18–21, 42, 61
Bosnian wars (1990s), 108
Bottollier, Marion, 100, 103, 152
Brănescu, Mimi, 52, 64, 97, 129, 151, 152
Brătilă, Mihai, 151, 152
Breathless (1960), 46
Brecht, Bertold, 1
Bresson, Robert, 1, 3, 133
bribery, 53–54, 56–57, 64, 66, 120n23
Bridges of Sarajevo (2014), 13, 107–8, 112, 115–16, 143–44; at Cannes Film Festival, 115–16, 134
Brooke, Michael, 65, 66, 71
Broussot, Ugo, 100, 102, 103, 152
Brown, John Murray, 111
Bruno, Giordano, 136–37
Bruno, Giuliana, 10, 30
"Bucharest, Bucharest" (song), 112
Bucur, Dragoş, 41–42, 50, 68, 97, 151, 152
Bunescu, Dana, 151, 152

Les Cahiers du Cinéma, 95, 143–44
Căliman, Calin, 22–26
Callas Forever (2002), 24
camera work: in *Aurora* (2010), 80–81, 84, 86–90, 93–94, 137; in *The Death of Mr. Lazarescu* (2005), 60, 62–63, 66–67, 128–29, 138; haptic imagery and, 5–6, 10, 28–31, 34, 47, 66–67; impact of camera-observer, 135–36, 137–38; in New Romanian Cinema (NRC), 27; in *The Retirement Home* (1998), 28–39; in *Stuff and Dough* (2001), 44, 47–48, 128–29
Camus, Albert, 74
Cannes Film Festival, 97; *Aurora* (2010), 85, 134; *Bridges of Sarajevo* (2014), 115–16, 134; *The Death of Mr. Lazarescu* (2005), 58; Palme d'Or, 58, 96; *Stuff and Dough* (2001), 1–2, 40, 50
Caragiale, Ion Luca, 113–14, 145
Caranfil, Nae, 24
Un cartuş de Kent şi un pachet de cafea. See *Cigarettes and Coffee* (2004)
Cassavetes, John, 3, 51, 123–24
Castel Films, 24
Caught in the Acts (1994), 135
Ceauşescu, Elena, 38–39, 52, 129, 149n4
Ceauşescu, Nicolae, 3, 14–18, 20, 38–39, 125, 146
The Celebration (1998), 139–40
censorship, 16, 17, 52, 146
Un Certain Regard award, 96, 97; *The Death of Mr. Lazarescu* (2005), 2
Les Chantiers Nomades, 98, 140–41, 152
Charles, Anne-Marie, 100, 102–3, 152
Chatman, Seymour, 92–93
Child's Pose (2013), 97
Chiriac, Dan, 152
Chirilov, Mihai, 2, 40, 42, 50, 141
Christian Democrat National Peasants' Party (CDNPP), 20, 146–47
The Chronicles of Pain (1991–1997), 26
Chronos, 33
Cigarettes and Coffee (2004), 43, 50–58, 129, **151**; camera work, 53–54; fathers and sons, 51–58, 129; Golden Bear Award (Berlin), 50–51, 58, 59, 124; "precariat"/capitalism in, 52–58; reviews, 58; summary, 11, 51–52
Cinerom, 22
Cioabă, Mirela, 152
Ciobanu, Luchian, 141, 152, 153
Civilization and Its Discontents (Freud), 104
Cleo from 5 to 7 (1962), 82
Coffee and Cigarettes (2003), 51
Colceag, Gelu, 75, 152
Cold Mountain (2002), 24
The Competition (1982), 16
Constantinescu, Emil, 19, 21, 127, 149n3
Constantinescu, Ştefan, 4, 127–28, 149n3
Corbul, Vintilă, 114
Corjos, Nicolae, 26
Costanzo, Leonardo di, 108
Costas, Pedro, 4
Courpron, Anne, 100, 152
Cowell, Alan, 107
Crime and Punishment (Dostoyevsky), 74
The Cruise (1981), 16
Culda, Carmela, 83

Daneliuc, Mircea, 16, 17
Danish Dogma 95, 4
Danquart, Didi, 60
Deaconeci, Mihaela, 151

death: in *The Death of Mr. Lazarescu* (2005), 8, 9, 60, 61, 66–67, 69, 70–72; in *The Retirement Home* (1998), 10, 33–34; in *Sieranevada* (2016), 8, 116, 118; in *Stuff and Dough* (2001), 8, 9, 48
The Death of Mr. Lazarescu (2005), 28, 30, 58–72, 82, 116, 127, 128–30, **152**; allegory in, 68–69; camera work, 60, 62–63, 66–67, 128–29, 138; at Cannes Film Festival, 58; Un Certain Regard award, 2; as cinematic realism, 1, 2, 4–5; compassion toward characters, 60–68, 69–71; controversy surrounding, 1, 58–59, 72; death in, 8, 9, 60, 61, 66–67, 69, 70–72; documentary approach in, 63–68; ethnographic "thick description" (Geertz) in, 63–68; "experiential" quality of, 6, 58–59; funding issues, 124–25; "minimalism" of, 4–5; origins of, 129–30; reviews, 58–59, 72; in *Six Tales from the Outskirts of Bucharest* series, 59–60, 124; as start of a "revolution" in film, 58–59; summary, 12, 60–62
The Death Triangle (1999), 23
deFilm, 152
Deletant, Dennis, 14–15, 18, 19, 77
Depardon, Raymond, 3, 28, 66, 135
De Vos, Susan, 61
Digital Cube, 152
Dilema (magazine), 141
Diță, Conastantin, 152
Djilas, Milovan, 14–15
Dogaru, Dana, 62, 152
Dostoyevsky, Fyodor, 74
Drăgănescu, Costica, 151
drug trafficking, 41–42
Dumitrache, Bogdan, 97, 152
Dumitrescu, Catrinel, 75, 152
Dumitrescu, Laura, 49
Dumitrescu, Mircea, 23

Eastern Orthodoxy, 7, 102, 116
École Supérieure d'Arts Visuels (Geneva), 1, 3, 27, 132
Eliade, Mircea, 8
ELO, 77
Elsaesser, Thomas, 74
ER (1994–2009), 68
Et in Arcadia Ego (Poussin), 115
EURIMAGES, 24, 73
Europe (Das Spektrum Europas) (Keyserling), 107–16, 144–45
European Union (EU), 6, 21, 73, 107–16
Euroskepticism, 107, 111–12
Eustache, Jean, 3, 124

Farocki, Harun, 18
fathers and children: *Aurora* (2010), 74–75, 78, 83–85, 89–90; *Cigarettes and Coffee* (2004), 51–58; *Stuff and Dough* (2001), 39–42, 44–45, 49, 53, 130
Ferencz-Flatz, Christian, 7, 106
Fieschi, Jean-André, 124
Filmex-România, 151
Film Studio of the Ministry of Culture, 22, 40, 151
financial crisis (2008), 6, 111
Fiscuteanu, Ioan, 60, 97, 129–30, 152
Flora, Ioana, 41, 97, 98, 151
Flutur, Cristina, 97
4 Months, 3 Weeks, and 2 Days (2007), 58, 96
French New Wave, 4
Freud, Sigmund, 104
Frodon, Jean-Michel, 107–8, 143–44
The Fury (2002), 97

Gaidenko, Piama, 105
Galilei, Galileo, 136–37
Galt, Rosalind, 23, 24–25
Geertz, Clifford, 12, 63
Gheorghe, Bogdan, 151
Gheorghiu, Luminița, 41, 60, 75, 97, 151, 152
Gide, André, 148
Gilbey, Ryan, 59, 60, 61, 65, 66
Giurgiu, Tudor, 59, 97
Gledhill, John, 76
Glissando (1984), 17
Godard, Jean-Luc, 108, 140
Golden Bear Award, 96–97; *Cigarettes and Coffee* (2004), 50–51, 58, 59, 124
Gorbachev, Mikhail, 146
Gorzo, Andrei, 5, 58, 59
Gradjević, Izeta, 152

The Graduates (1986), 26
Guffroy, Perrine, 100, 152
Gulag (Romanian), 4, 104, 147. See also *The Archive of Pain* (2000)
Gulea, Stere, 16, 17, 25–26, 52, 129
guns, 75, 81, 82–83, 86–87, 88, 94
Gurescu, George, 26
Gusejnova, Dina, 109
Gusyatinskiy, Evgeny, 141
The Gypsy Baron (operetta), 144

Hamlet (Shostakovich), 90
Henley, Jon, 107
High School Rock 'n' Roll (1992), 23, 26
Hill, Steven, 107
Hirsch, Marianne, 37
Hoberman, Jim, 6, 66, 68, 72
Hockenos, Paul, 107
Holden, Stephen, 60, 66
Hospital (1970), 66
Hossu-Longin, Lucia, 26
Hristescu, Tudor, 152
Hughes, Kirsty, 107
hyperrealism, 132

Ianoşi, Ion, 98
If I Want to Whistle, I Whistle (2010), 97
Iiescu, Ion, 19–21, 26, 146
Imre, Anikó, 15
Ionesco, Eugène, 71
Ionescu, Cristina, 151
I, Pierre Rivière (1976), 74
irony, 113–15

Jarmusch, Jim, 51, 53, 129
Jaspers, Karl, 25
Jeanne Dielman, 23 Quai du Commerce, 1080 Bruxelles (1983), 82
Jude, Radu, 24
Judt, Tony, 14, 18, 19
July 13th–July 19th, 1998 (13–19 iulie 1998, Craiova, Azilul de bătrâni). See *The Retirement Home* (1998)
justice, 147–48

Kalev, Kamen, 108
Käppner, Joachim, 107
Kaurismäki Aki, 133
Keegin, Hillary, 100, 104, 105, 152
Keyserling, Hermann, 107–16, 144–45
Kiarostami, Abbas, 4, 140
The King and the Corpse (Zimmer), 102
King, Charles, 76
Korzybski, Alfred, 102
Kotkin, Stephen, 14, 17
Kubrick, Stanley, 30
Kurosawa, Akira, 123

Lanzmann, Claude, 26
The Last Ball in November (1989), 17
Lazăr, Rodica, 152
Léaud, Jean-Pierre, 143
Le Besco, Islid, 108
Led Zeppelin, 77
Lefebvre, Henri, 29
"The Little Ewe," 69
Little Red Riding Hood (Perrault), 82–83
love, 13, 59–60, 103–6
Loznitsa, Sergei, 108
Lumière brothers, 95
Lungu, Adrian, 111

Magna, Leptis, 29
Mamet, David, 13, 106, 137
Mandragora, 59, 116, 149n5, 152
Marfa şi banii (2001). See *Stuff and Dough* (2001)
Marjanović, Jovan, 152
Marra, Vincenzo, 108
Masci, Raffaello, 107
masks, 13, 106
Matta Almeida, Luis da, 108
Mazierska, Ewa, 76, 78
MEDIA (Measures to Encourage the Development of the Audio Visual Industries), 73
MediaPro, 24
Meier, Ursula, 108
Metamorphosis (Ovid), 40
Meunier, Nathalie, 100, 152
Michaelson, Annette, 30
Microphone Test (1980), 16, 17
Mihăileanu, Radu, 24
Mihăilescu, Ionel, 52, 129
Ministry of Culture (Romania), 22, 40, 59, 73

Miss Litoral (1990), 26
Mitchievici, Angelo, 4, 25
Mitulescu, Cătălin, 24, 58, 59, 97
Moartea domnului Lăzărescu (2005). See *The Death of Mr. Lazarescu (2005)*
The Moromete Family (1987), 17, 52, 129
The Mother and the Whore (1973), 124, 143
Mr. Lazarescu. See *The Death of Mr. Lazarescu* (2005)
Mr. Leonida Faces the Reactionaries (Caragiale), 113–14, 145
Mungiu, Cristian, 16, 51, 58, 59, 73, 96, 97
Muntean, Radu, 16, 23, 58, 73, 74, 97
Munteanu, Alexandru, 59, 152
Muresan, Mircea, 26
Murnau, F. W., 80–81
Mutu, Oleg, 66, 129–30, 151, 152
Mystery Train (1989), 53

Nasta, Dominique, 4–5
National Center for Cinematography (NCC), 22, 40, 51, 59, 72–73, 116, 124, 125, 151
National Cinema Fund, 23
National University of Theater and Film "I. L. Caragiale" (Bucharest), 3, 22, 97
Neagu, Alina, 111
Netzer, Călin Peter, 24, 97
New Romanian Cinema (NRC): birth of the antihero, 78–79; funding issues, 2, 22–24, 40, 59, 72–74, 116, 124–25; key features of, 2, 4, 97, 113–14; "minimalism" of, 4–5; origins of, 14, 20, 51, 124, 125; "traditional" Romanian cinema *versus,* 4, 16–17, 22–24, 51, 58–59, 72–73, 124
Nica, Constantin, 60
Nicolaescu, Sergiu, 51
Niki and Flo (2003), 60
Notes sur le cinématographe (Bresson), 1
"nothingness," 51–52
NRC (New Romanian Cinema). *See* New Romanian Cinema

Obala Art Centar, 152
Occident (2002), 97
Offset (2006), 60
On Directing Film (Mamet), 137
O'Neill, Eugene, 147
Oroveanu, Mihai, 128
Ovid, 40

Păduraru, Andreea, 10, 27–39, 126–27, 151
Palme d'Or, 58, 96
Paludes (Marshlands) (Gide), 148
Panahi, Jafar, 106
Panduru, Marius, 126–27, 151
Papacioc, Arsenie, 102, 104, 147–48, 149n11
Papadopol, Alexandru, 40–42, 97, 151
The Paper Will Be Blue (2006), 58–59
Paramount, 24
Păunescu, Bobby, 152
Pavlu, Şerban, 152
peace, 104, 147–48
Perisic, Vladimir, 108
Perlez, Jane, 21
Péron, Didier, 72
Perrault, Charles, 83
Perrotey, Barnabé, 100, 106, 152
Petre, Dorotheea, 97
Petrescu, Gică, 112
Philanthropy (2000), 24
photorealism, 132
Pink Floyd, 46
Pinter, Harold, 98
Pintilie, Lucian, 16, 22, 40, 60
Pîrvulescu, Cristian, 107
Piţa, Dan, 16, 17
Piteşti experiment, or Phenomenon, 147, 149n10
Plato, 136
Plazy, Frédéric, 140
Poirier, Jean-Benoît, 100, 102, 103, 152
Police, Adjective (2009), 73, 96, 97
Les Ponts de Sarajevo. See *Bridges of Sarajevo* (2014)
Pop, Doru, 5, 6–7, 49, 54, 57, 58, 64, 74, 78, 117
Popescu, Cristian Tudor, 16
Popescu, Simona, 152
Popescu, Valentin, 75, 152
Porumboiu, Corneliu, 58, 73, 74, 96, 97

Poussin, Nicolas, 115
precariat classes: in *Aurora* (2010), 75–80; in *Cigarettes and Coffee* (2004), 52–58; in *Sieranevada* (2016), 116–17; in *Stuff and Dough* (2001), 11, 14, 42–47, 50, 53–54
Pricop, Lucian, 24, 59
Princip, Gavrilo, 108
Puiu, Anca (wife), 59, 130, 149n5, 152
Puiu, Cristi: on acting, 142–43; as "angry young director," 58, 72; in Christian-Democrat National Peasants' Party (CDNPP), 20, 146–47; cinematic philosophy of, 5–9, 93, 96, 99–100, 102, 104–6, 148 (*see also names of specific films*); on cinematic realism, 1–2, 3, 8–9, 132–33; compassion toward characters, 49–50, 60–71; "confessional" approach of, 6–7, 13, 148; discharge from army in 1990, 146; at École Supérieure d'Arts Visuels (Geneva), 1, 3, 27, 132; family background, 15; and fiction cinema, 6–7, 25; filmmaker influences on, 3, 16, 28, 51–52, 66, 72, 80–81, 82, 123–24, 129; films of (*see* Puiu films); on history, 145–48; hospital experiences, 60, 130; "ineffable"/sense of sacred dimension, 2, 7–9, 13, 93, 104–6, 131; interview, 96, 123–49; and NCC restructuring, 72–73, 124; on peace and justice, 147–48; in the Pioneers, 146, 149n9; return to Romania (1996), 3, 27–28; and Romanian revolution of 1989, 18–19, 145–48; television work, 28
Puiu films: *The Archive of Pain* (2000), 4, 127–28; *Aurora* (2010), 72–96, 133–35, **152**; *Before Breakfast* (student film), 147; *Cigarettes and Coffee* (2004), 50–58, **151**; *The Death of Mr. Lazarescu* (2005), 58–72, 128–30, **152**; *The Retirement Home* (1998), 27–39, 129–30, **151**; *Sieranevada* (2016), 8, 116–18, 149n8; *"Das Spektrum Europas"* (2014 short), 107–16, 143–48, **152–53**; *Stuff and Dough* (2001), 39–50, **151**; *Three Exercises of Interpretation* (2011), 98–106, 140–43, **152**
Puiu, Ileana (daughter), 82
Purivatra, Mirsad, 143–44, 152

Quandt, James, 65, 66, 71
Quinn, Ben, 107

Radio Free Europe, 147
Radu, Raluca-Nicoleta, 21, 23, 26, 59, 72
Rădulescu, Răzvan, 40–42, 60, 72, 124, 151, 152
Râlea, Marian, 108–9, 153
reason, role of, 136–37
Rebel Without a Cause (1955), 46
Rebengiuc, Victor, 52, 129, 151
Recha, Marc, 108
The Retirement Home (1998), 27–39, 43, 53, 60, 65, 129–30, **151**; camera work, 28–39; death in, 10, 33–34; as emotional journey through history, 28–30, 36–39; expectations about subjects of film, 35–36; haptic imagery and, 10, 28–31, 34; memory and storytelling in, 36–39; origins of project, 126–27; as participatory documentary, 27, 36–39; solidarity within the institution, 34–35; space and memory in, 29–32; statistics about the home, 31; summary, 10; time as giant washing machine metaphor, 32–34
Reverchon, Antoine, 107
Revue Sketches (Pinter), 98
Rofilm, 22, 40, 151
Rohmer, Eric, 3, 140
Roman, Denise, 42, 46
Romania: under Ceauşescu, 14–16; censorship in, 16, 17, 52, 146; condemnation of communism (2006), 72–73, 77; under Constantinescu, 19, 21, 127, 149n3; in financial crisis of 2008, 6, 111; Gulag, 4, 104, 147 (see also *The Archive of Pain* [2000]); under Iliescu, 19–21, 26; joins the European Union (EU), 6, 21, 73, 111; Ministry of Culture, 22, 40, 59, 73; national television, 23–24, 26; need for cultural policy, 125; New Romanian Cinema (*see* New Romanian Cinema [NRC]); post-revolution conditions in, 9–10; "precariat"/capitalism in, 11, 14, 42–47, 50, 52–58, 75–80, 111; Proposition #8,

19–20; retirees/pensioners in, 61; revolution of December, 1989, 3, 6, 17–19, 20, 25–26, 145–48; "traditional" cinema in, 4, 16–17, 22–24, 51, 58–59, 72–73, 124; University Square protests (1990), 19–20, 25–26, 147
Romanian Film Festival, 140
Romanian Filmmakers' Union, 50, 72
Rotterdam International Film Festival, 98, 141
Run Lola Run (1998), 74

Sábato, Ernesto, 74
Sakalauskaite, Diana, 100, 104, 106, 152
Şalapă, Katia, 151
Sand Cliffs (1983), 16
Sandefur, Gary, 61
Sandu, Ana Maria, 2, 40, 42, 50
Sarajevo Film Festival, 143–44
Sava, Valerian, 25, 26, 40, 49, 50, 51, 59, 72–73
Schanalec, Angela, 108
Schuiten, François, 108
Seciu, Valeria, 75, 108–9, 152, 153
The Second Fall of Constantinople (1994), 26
Seinfeld (1989–1998), 52
Sequences (1982), 16, 17
Şerban, Alex. Leo, 2, 4, 25, 46, 49–50, 58–59, 72
Şerban, Florin, 96–97
Sergovici, Viorel, 101, 152
sex and sexuality, 25–27, 79, 84–87
Shoah (1985), 26
A Short Organum for the Theater (Brecht), 1
Short Story of the Antichrist (Solovyov), 141
Shostakovich, Dmitri, 90
Sieranevada (2016), 116–18, 149n8; death in, 8, 116, 118; female characters, 116–17; in *Six Tales from the Outskirts of Bucharest* series, 116
Sitaru, Adrian, 24
Six Tales from the Outskirts of Bucharest series: Aurora (2010), 74; *The Death of Mr. Lazarescu* (2005), 59–60, 124; *Sieranevada* (2016), 116; synopses, 124
Sklar, Robert, 66
Sobchack, Vivian, 93, 96
Solomon, Alexandru, 24
Solovyov, Vladimir, 98–105, 141, 142, 152
Sontag, Susan, 12, 63–64
Spahiu, Gabriel, 68, 97, 152
"Das Spektrum Europas" (2014 short), 13, 107–16, **152–53**; character construction, 113–15; city as central metaphor, 112–13; classifications in, 109–10; films within, 108; irony, 113–15; memory and storytelling in, 115; origins of plot, 143–48; summary, 108–9
Standing, Guy, 11, 43
Stavilă, Silviu, 128, 151
Steefel, Lawrence D., Jr., 115
Stoica, Ion, 152
Stoica, Remus, 151
The Stranger (Camus), 74
Stranger than Paradise (1984), 51, 129
Stratan, Cosmina, 97
Stroe, Ioachim, 152, 153
Stuff and Dough (2001), 39–50, 82, 97–98, 123–24, **151**; camera work, 44, 47–48, 128–29; at Cannes Film Festival, 1–2, 40, 50; as cinematic realism, 1–2, 4; compassion toward characters, 49–50; death in, 8, 9, 48; fathers and sons, 39–42, 44–45, 49, 53, 130; "precariat"/capitalism in, 11, 14, 42–47, 50, 53–54; as Puiu debut feature, 1–2, 40, 50; release at Cannes Film Festival, 1–2, 40, 50; reviews, 1–2, 49–50; as road movie/initiation journey, 40–42, 45–49; Rofilm production problems, 22, 40; summary, 10–11, 40–42
Styx River, 33, 68, 71
Suciu, Oana-Valentina, 21
Sunrise (1927), 80–81
surrealism, 133

Tales from the Golden Age (2009), 97
Tatos, Alexandru, 16
television, 23–24, 26, 28, 74, 127, 144, 146; *The Chronicles of Pain* (1991–1997), 26; *ER* (1994–2009), 68; *Seinfeld* (1989–1998), 52
Temple Film, 151

The 10th District Court: Judicial Hearings (2004), 135
Theodorescu, Răzvan, 59
Thick description (Geertz), 12, 63–68, 83
13–19 iulie, Craiova, Azilul de bătrâni (July 13th–July 19th, Craiova). See *The Retirement Home* (1998)
Thompson, James, 115
Three Conversations (Solovyov), 98–105, 141, 142
Three Exercises of Interpretation (2011), 98–106, **152**; origins and development, 98, 140–43; summary, 13, 100–104
Tismaneanu, Vladimir, 14–15, 19, 21
Titieni, Adrian, 68, 152
Tolstoy, Leo, 99
Traffic (2004), 58
Transylvania International Film Festival (TIFF), 72, 141
Traynor, Ian, 107
Trois exercices d'interprétation. See *Three Exercises of Interpretation* (2011)
Truffaut, François, 140
trust, 124
truth, 103–6, 142–43
Tuesday, After Christmas (2010), 74, 97
The Tunnel (Sábato), 74
Ţuţea, Petre, 102
12:08 East of Bucharest (2006), 58
2001: A Space Odyssey (1968), 30

Ujică, Andrei, 18
University Square protests (1990), 19–20, 25–26, 147
University Square-Romania (1991), 25–26
Uricaru, Ioana, 16, 22, 23, 24, 40

Vaillant, Patrick, 100, 152
Varda, Agnés, 82
Varendoe, Kirk, 5
Vasilescu, Razvan, 151
Verdery, Katherine, 10, 14–15, 19, 21, 53
Videogames of a Revolution (1992), 18
Villaverde, Teresa, 108
Vodă, Clara, 68, 74–75, 134, 152

The Wall (album), 46
The Way I Spent the End of the World (2006), 97
Weerasethakul, Apichatpong, 106
What is Cinema? (Bazin), 147
When Evening Falls on Bucharest or Metabolism (2013), 74, 97
Why Are the Bells Ringing, Mitica? (1981), 16
Why is Romania Different? (Boia), 13–14
Wilde, Kim, 61
Williams, Alan, 91
Wiseman, Frederick, 3, 28, 66, 72
Wollen, Peter, 95–96
A Woman Under the Influence (1974), 51, 123
World War I, 107–8, 109, 112, 113, 143–44
World War II, 24, 38, 95, 109

xenophobia, 13, 111–12

Zamfirescu, Florin, 152
Zhangke, Jia, 140
Zimmer, Heinrich, 102
Žižek, Slavoj, 76

Monica Filimon is an assistant professor of English at Kingsborough Community College, CUNY.

Books in the series Contemporary Film Directors

Nelson Pereira dos Santos
Darlene J. Sadlier

Abbas Kiarostami
Mehrnaz Saeed-Vafa and Jonathan Rosenbaum

Joel and Ethan Coen
R. Barton Palmer

Claire Denis
Judith Mayne

Wong Kar-wai
Peter Brunette

Edward Yang
John Anderson

Pedro Almodóvar
Marvin D'Lugo

Chris Marker
Nora Alter

Abel Ferrara
Nicole Brenez, translated by Adrian Martin

Jane Campion
Kathleen McHugh

Jim Jarmusch
Juan Suárez

Roman Polanski
James Morrison

Manoel de Oliveira
John Randal Johnson

Neil Jordan
Maria Pramaggiore

Paul Schrader
George Kouvaros

Jean-Pierre Jeunet
Elizabeth Ezra

Terrence Malick
Lloyd Michaels

Sally Potter
Catherine Fowler

Atom Egoyan
Emma Wilson

Albert Maysles
Joe McElhaney

Jerry Lewis
Chris Fujiwara

Jean-Pierre and Luc Dardenne
Joseph Mai

Michael Haneke
Peter Brunette

Alejandro González Iñárritu
Celestino Deleyto and Maria del Mar Azcona

Lars von Trier
Linda Badley

Hal Hartley
Mark L. Berrettini

François Ozon
Thibaut Schilt

Steven Soderbergh
Aaron Baker

Mike Leigh
Sean O'Sullivan

D.A. Pennebaker
Keith Beattie

Jacques Rivette
Mary M. Wiles

Kim Ki-duk
Hye Seung Chung

Philip Kaufman
Annette Insdorf

Richard Linklater
David T. Johnson

David Lynch
Justus Nieland

John Sayles
David R. Shumway

Dario Argento
L. Andrew Cooper

Todd Haynes
Rob White

Christian Petzold
Jaimey Fisher

Spike Lee
Todd McGowan

Terence Davies
Michael Koresky

Francis Ford Coppola
Jeff Menne

Emir Kusturica
Giorgio Bertellini

Agnès Varda
Kelley Conway

John Lasseter
Richard Neupert

Paul Thomas Anderson
George Toles

Cristi Puiu
Monica Filimon

The University of Illinois Press
is a founding member of the
Association of American University Presses.

University of Illinois Press
1325 South Oak Street
Champaign, IL 61820-6903
www.press.uillinois.edu